AF352308

MISSION 2009

The Future of the Catholic Church in the South

Edited by
John S. Rausch

50th Aniversary Symposium of the Glenmary Home Missioners

Published by Glenmary Research Center
Atlanta, Georgia 30308

Libarary of Congress Catalogue Number: 90080047
ISBN: 0-914422-19-7

CONTENTS

ACKNOWLEDGEMENTS

I acknowledge with sincere thanks the many hands and hearts that cooperated to produce Mission 2009, the symposium as well as the book. Glenmary members with support staff in Cincinnati and Atlanta coordinated efforts across the miles to produce a program highly praised by the participants in August, 1989. I hope this book which presents the major addresses of that symposium is received with the same enthusiasm.

The Glenmary council, Frank Ruff president, deserves recognition for proposing the symposium as an appropriate expression for the society's fiftieth anniversary. The council's choice of speakers insured an excellent program. James P. Kelly with the help of the anniversary committee, which he chaired, graciously dealt with a myriad of financial details relating to the symposium while his committee oversaw other commemorative events throughout the year. Most of all Dan Dorsey, my faithful partner and brother, helped shoulder the sundry details of the symposium that guaranteed a solid program and a comfortable time for all the participants. We were a good team.

I thank Mary May with her red pen in hand who shared editorial duties and offered her sharp eye for proofreading. Other staff at the Glenmary Research Center deserve thanks for adding their skills at the computer to produce this volume.

Discerning the future of the church remains a daunting task, so my deepest thanks go to the resource people and presenters at the symposium whose thoughts are contained in this volume. With their ideas and inspiration, the church can anticipate a renewal for mission through a commitment to honest dialogue with the cultures of the south.

John S. Rausch, Editor

INTRODUCTION

Spacious green fields, some dotted with livestock, spread in all directions where three hundred participants gathered for *Mission 2009: Birthing the Church Among Southern Peoples*. The rural scene, located at Eastern Kentucky University, offered a natural symbol for the convocation. The southern population, predominately small town and rural yet affected by new migration trends, views its culture as both distinct from and in many ways common with the rest of the nation. To evangelize among southern peoples a missioner must understand and appreciate the unique distinctions. The symposium contrasted several expressions of culture in the South with one another and those in the Catholic Church as a whole.

Mission 2009, held in August, 1989, capped a year of celebration marking the fiftieth anniversary of the Glenmary Home Missioners of America. Looking at the next twenty years—which loaned the number 2009 to the title—the symposium intertwined evangelization and ecumenism, and highlighted striking questions on cross-cultural concerns.

The papers collected in this volume point to some of the questions the church must consider if it wants to be assimilated into southern culture and the sub-groups of that culture. At best *Mission 2009* focused issues and defined terms. It sought to discuss cultural differences in a holistic way through expressions of song, dance and other participant involvement throughout the program.

What occasioned this symposium on the future of the Church in the South? Who are its sponsors, the Glenmary Home Missioners of America? What are the issues dealing with cross-cultural evangelization in this region? And finally, how do these collected papers address the symposium's purpose and need for the church to become inculturated in the South? These questions are like the white rail fences that break the fields and add relief to the landscape of that rural state university, These questions offer some logical divisions for assessing how the Catholic church—long viewed as a northern church—can become a church *in* the South and *of* the South.

The Glenmary Symposium

To celebrate its Golden Jubilee, Glenmary convened a symposium about the future of Catholic evangelization in the South. The doors swung open to women and co-ministers, to representatives from Catholic dioceses across the nation and to Protestant brothers and sisters. All participants were welcomed to share creative threads for weaving a mission tapestry that would express evangelization in the South for the next twenty years.

The Glenmary Home Missioners is a religious society of ninety priests and Brothers dedicated to serving small towns and rural areas in Appalachia and the South. Its mission plan calls it to establish the Catholic church where it is not effectively present, and then move on. This missionary work is the essential purpose of Glenmary.

Father Frank Ruff, the president of Glenmary, stated that although Glenmary had a half century of experience, the Church and society had changed. "We need help," he admitted humbly, "to know how to be true to ourselves, to the people of the home missions, and to the larger church."

For five decades Glenmary pursued evangelization undauntedly as native-to-native mission work. This "like to like" ministry formed the basis of Glenmary's concept of home missions. Although Glenmary priests and Brothers received a steady trickle of converts, over the years Glenmary parishes grew primarily by accretion—northern and cradle Catholics migrated into the parish. Few inroads were cut to the indigenous people. Fr. Frank Ruff, speaking for Glenmary and the church's entire mission effort in the South, honestly admitted, "...we do not do cross-cultural evangelization well."

Instinctively Glenmary always demonstrated a sensitivity to identify with people, and especially with society's neglected people. Glenmary's mystique revolved around the small and the rural, the ability to rub shoulders with anyone and relate to local folks. By choosing ministry in small towns Glenmary adopted a manner of simplicity in dealing with people, clear, clean and uncluttered. To that spontaneous gesture of outreach, *Mission 2009* wedded the critical perspectives from the social sciences.

The symposium posited the principle that in America, despite its great melting pot imagery, evangelization requires a specific assessment of various groups with their unique experiences as a prelude to hearing the gospel.

While Glenmary's fiftieth anniversary occasioned *Mission 2009*, the fundamental objective of the symposium was to define the contemporary issues of mission. The candid appraisals of previous efforts that proved less than effective did not stifle the enthusiasm to find a deeper understanding of evangelization. The outcome of the symposium demonstrated that authentic evangelization occurs when missioners appreciate the historic moment of the local people and address God's

Word in that context. That approach creates the framework for dialogue, the essential tool of the missioner.

Cross-Cultural Considerations

The planners of *Mission 2009* believed that cross-cultural considerations held the key to unlock a new burst of energy for evangelization in the South. The symposium highlighted the region's three principal cultural groups—African-Americans, Hispanics and white Protestants.

Sr. Jamie Phelps reminded the symposium of the definition of evangelization contained in **Evangelii Nuntiandi**, Paul VI's encyclical of 1975. Evangelization is the process of "bringing Good News into all the strata of humankind and through its influence transforming from within and making it new..." The purpose of evangelization is the "interior change...of the personal and collective consciousness of people, the activities in which they engage and the lives and concrete milieux which are theirs." Summarized, this concept of evangelization calls for social as well as personal transformation.

Historically while mission groups acknowledged cultural differences between themselves and the people to whom they were sent, missioners emphasized the analysis of how *individuals* receive a message. A missioner learned that a listener's interpretation of the message is based on personal needs and background, plus an ability to understand the symbols and to process the message into a system of meaning. Missioners rarely focused sufficiently on the culture itself that nurtured the system of meaning, behavior and values of its people.

A key insight of mission practice recognizes that people are best addressed in their specific cultural circumstances. Hence, the effective communication of a message makes use of the characteristics of those sub-cultural groups.

The message of evangelization will be heard principally in two ways: through the cultural paradigm of the people; and through the actions of the evangelizer.

The challenge missioners face is to incorporate the cultural paradigms of each sub-group in the process of proclaiming the Good News. As the Exodus became the paradigmatic event of the Jews for their comprehending God, so did slavery evolve as the most significant event for African-Americans. "Our understanding of Jesus is that of Jesus the Liberator," said Sr. Jamie Phelps. "You got to change your language, your attitude and your world vision, if you want to know how to evangelize southern blacks."

Sr. Yolanda Tarango, addressing the situation of Hispanics, stressed, "The primary symbol of Hispanic evangelization is captured in the image of Guadalupe." It was the respect the woman gave to Juan Diego, a peasant, that affirmed his worth, thus counteracting the contempt from society that demeaned his culture and denied his worth.

Dr. Bill Leonard, looking at southern white evangelical cultures, referred to the Civil War and its aftermath as the source of meaning for those cultures. For Leonard the Great Southern Myth was this: "The people who lost the war retained the vision. The defeated people, even in defeat, would be more gracious, more resourceful, and more communal than their Yankee counterparts could ever be."

These three distinct paradigms arising from the history and experience of the people transform evangelization from technique to understanding. They discount the notion that evangelization represents one solitary approach, and beckon the missioner to continue the dialogue relating to cross-cultural questions.

Yet, besides appreciating the cultural paradigms, the *actions* of missioners in approaching the receptor group also determine how the message is heard. Into whatever community or culture they go, missioners will choose to associate with a certain local class, either the haves or the have-nots. They will choose either to cling to their privileges, or surrender them to identify with the struggles of the common people for dignity and liberation. Missioners sometimes approach a community with answers, with programs and with irresistible resources. They can either foster dependency or encourage self-determination. From their initial appearance the proclamation of the message will be affected by the disposition of the missioners.

The attitude that affirms dignity and promotes liberation, on the other hand, reflects a disposition of commitment to the host culture. The missioners see themselves as resources for the community, participants who encourage the development of indigenous leadership, while standing in long-term solidarity with the community facing its struggle for redemptive wholeness. In this regard cross-cultural work authentically involves a mutuality in mission whereby missioners act on what people say while accepting a servant role. Evangelization that leads to liberation recognizes the Holy Spirit already present in every culture. Sr. Yolanda Tarango in her paper refers to the programs aimed at evangelizing Hispanics that disregard the deep sense of faith nurtured for hundreds of years, as often patronizing and alienating. In light of this deeper understanding, can evangelization that furthers dependency and disregards social transformation effectively promote full conversion, heart and soul, on the personal level?

The Symposium Papers

All the speakers at *Mission 2009* had the common objective to envision the church twenty years in the future. Each contributed insights on evangelization and cross-cultural challenges.

Three questions help summarize the collected papers of this volume. How can the church evangelize more effectively in the South? What role will it play in the development of people and the liberation of cultural groups? Who of the church has the clearest opportunity to evangelize? These three questions catalogue the insights for this introduction while they guide the reader through the rest of the book.

The first question deals with the church's ability to evangelize more effectively in the South. Some speakers envision a different Catholic Church altogether. Fr. Frank Ruff supports a vision for the church that is born of the southern culture, a church "*in* the South and *of* the South." This inculturation reflects the title of the symposium: birthing the church among southern peoples. Cardinal Bernardin affirms that same need when he says, "...Catholics will have to be *fully southern*, as well as *fully Catholic*." At stake are issues of faithfulness to the tradition and openness to change.

Liturgical expressions will require greater flexibility to engage people of diverse paradigms and experiences. Sr. Jamie Phelps links participation of African-Americans in parish decision making with patterns of liturgical inculturation as a further expression of cultural respect. Dr. Bill Leonard argues for a Catholic liturgy that blends the sacramental and pietistic—"heart religion nurtured on powerful symbols of the church..." He also recognizes that "lay participation in worship is essential in Appalachia," and he encourages Catholic evangelism to be "unabashedly biblical in its public expression."

Sr. Yolanda Tarango contrasts the mainstream model of evangelization emphasizing individual conversion and knowledge with the Hispanic cultures' method of evangelizating "through feeling and example." Popular religion preserved the faith and traditions of the ancestors. The church will evangelize among Hispanics more effectively when it appreciates the manifestations of popular religion that encourage novenas, processions, *altarcitos* (home altars), and other cherished expressions of devotion.

A final theme for effective Catholic evangelization in the South coupled renewal with resources. Cardinal Bernardin, as an able church administrator, pointed to the wise use of resources as proper stewardship for a minority group like the Catholic Church. Sharing responsibility with lay people—women as well as men—becomes essential for Catholic education and increasingly for parish life itself. Joe Holland pushed the idea further by sensing the need for a lay-inspired renewal to dislodge clericalism and to rediscover the inclusiveness of the Greek term *laos*, the word for "laity," which means "God's own chosen, holy, royal, and priestly people."

To evangelize more effectively in the South, the church must reflect a flexibility to change in order to dialogue with the culture it is called to serve.

The second question asks what role the church will play in the development and liberation of people and their culture. A prophetic dialogue emerged as a way to affirm the goodness and truth of a culture while challenging the oppressive structures. Sr. Jamie Phelps offered a mission model that first accepts all people as they are (living in God's love,) then critiques the culture's inhumane structures (sinfulness) and finally moves to a new and transformed culture (new life.) The model reflects Christ's Incarnation, Death and Resurrection, respectively. The third stage, transformation, evolves from a Christian critique to a whole new expression unanticipated in the beginning by either the host culture or the Christian evangelizer.

For specific groups the Catholic community offers a potential for healing cultural narrowness and strengthening greater cooperation. Dr. Bill Leonard encourages Catholics to participate in the renewal of a theology of evangelism that skirts the shortcomings of both nineteenth century evangelicalism and sacramentalism. That new synthesis between Catholic and Protestant evangelization depends on trust and understanding. To initiate this process he suggests "Catholic evangelism in Appalachia begin with presence and service."

Sr.Yolanda Tarango emphasizes that evangelization with Hispanics must acknowledge the traditional values that created a unique identity as both Catholic and Hispanic in a dominant United States culture. She envisions the eventual third stage synthesis requiring support of the family with some type of "creative continuity of rituals and symbols that have expressed Hispanic faith for many generations."

On the broadest plain the liberation and development of people assume a more traditionally prophetic mode. Fr. Frank Ruff raises a voice for those who have no voice in the Catholic Church. He challenges the church to take seriously the "155 counties in the rural South in which there is still no Catholic presence of any kind—no faith community, no Catholic worship, no Catholic minister." Cardinal Bernardin cites prevailing cultural values that must be challenged—consumerism, materialism and secularism. Social justice issues may also demand attention in a particular sub-culture, especially racism, unfair labor practices and violence in all its forms. Joe Holland sketches an anti-ecological addiction in Western culture destined to kill mother earth unless it is stopped. To this he adds social parallels "which have their distinct but linked dynamics, especially the oppressions of racism, sexism, classism, and ageism (including the attack on the unborn.)"

To stand with the process of liberation and development of culture requires an acceptance, a critique and finally a transformation of people and their structures.

The final question asks who has the best opportunity to evangelize in the South. The obvious answer, the laity, needs clarification. Cardinal Bernardin demonstrated statistically that while the Catholic population of the South increased by 425,486 in the past twenty years, the net increase of priests serving the region was a paltry 17. He credibly predicts "the church in the South will have to rely increasingly upon lay leadership." Joe Holland rejoices in that future provided the church returns to an apostolic model of a lay community containing various ministries without the religious elitism and clericalism that block responsibility for the love and power of the gospel.

Sr. Yolanda Tarango recognizes that authentic evangelization proceeds from the family in Hispanic cultures. "Traditionally the family has played a critical role in evangelizing generations of Hispanics." She emphasizes the need to support that primal institution especially with the weakening of the Hispanic family in the United States. While the family is losing influence in the evangelization of younger generations, the role of the family remains significant for proclaiming the faith.

Dr. Bill Leonard observes that among white Protestants a gentle presence emphasizing service is the starting point of Catholic evangelization. He commends the witness of religious women who frequently come to a new region to "be with people" as the most effective way to dispel anti-Catholic bigotry and build trust.

Lamenting that social justice is treated separately from evangelization, Sr. Jamie Phelps suggests a model that blends the two. The Catholic Committee of the South (CCS) unites with non-church related groups to address social and political struggles for justice. The non-church groups take the lead in designating the justice issues, but CCS interjects a reflective dimension that places the process of liberation in a faith context. The mutuality and dialogue becomes a strong example of authentic evangelization.

While affirming the role of lay ministry in evangelization, Fr. Frank Ruff transforms the question from the "who" of evangelization to the "how long" of evangelization. For fifty years Glenmary ministered in populations that were less than one per cent Catholic along side other dedicated religious men and women. Whoever comes to evangelize in the South faces a long term commitment of presence, service and love.

The symposium speakers answered the three questions by offering no blueprint for evangelization, no set of techniques, no bag of tricks. Their insights highlighted salient aspects of culture that expanded the dialogue about God's Word and message. They informed, but mostly they inspired.

A Final Word

Evangelization has a dynamism that encompasses a wide range of activities. Digressing from her prepared text, Sr. Jamie Phelps epitomized evangelization when she said, "Don't offer people bread if you aren't willing to offer them Eucharist." Speaking forthrightly about liberation as "a component part of evangelization," Sr. Jamie offered a sensitive balance between convert making and social activism. Authentic evangelization addresses the entire human situation with its sinfulness, brokenness and oppression. To the extent the human heart needs freedom in social or political ways, the gospel promises a vision for a fuller life within society. To the degree that loneliness, alienation and guilt grip the soul, the gospel offers the liberation of forgiveness and healing for one's personal spirit. Plainly put, evangelization invites everyone into the community of believers to struggle for the renewal of society and the personal development of the spirit. If this is the evangelization that authentically engages the culture of the South, then twenty years hence the church of the South will be indigenous. Formed by this evangelization, the Church of the South will then send missioners to initiate the process of re-evangelization in the North and beyond.

John S. Rausch, Editor
April, 1990

I

A VISION OF THE CHURCH IN THE SOUTH AND OF THE SOUTH IN 2009

Joseph Cardinal Bernardin

Cardinal Bernardin, a native of the South, first discusses the trends in the demography, religion and politics of the South before placing the Catholic church in that context. His vision of the Church in the South allows for mutual influence between church and culture. Pointing to the future he enumerates seven ways the church can become fully southern and fully Catholic.

The topic of this presentation is close to my heart— the South and the Church in the South.

However, after I agreed to deliver the address and reflected on what was expected of me, I began to think that, perhaps, I should have *hesitated* before accepting or even *declined* the invitation. Let me explain my scruple.

First, I've ministered outside the South for more than twenty years. I left Atlanta and moved to Washington, D.C., in July, 1968. While the nation's capital has historical roots in the South, today it defies any regional identification. Moreover, my responsibilities there as General Secretary of the NCCB/USCC had a *national* scope. Then, in December, 1972, I moved to Cincinnati—and, in 1982, to Chicago. This means that my knowledge and experience of the changes of the past two decades in the South are secondhand for the most part.

Moreover, as I thought about the assigned topic, I became more aware of the difficulty, indeed the impossibility, of looking twenty years into the future—to 2009, as the title of the address promises. Much of what has happened in the past two decades was quite unforeseen. For example, twenty years ago, in 1969, we observed the first anniversary of Dr. Martin Luther King Jr.'s assassination and pondered the gloomy future of the civil rights movement. Last year, Rev. Jesse Jackson mounted a serious effort to be President of the United States. We clearly have a long way to go in regard to civil rights, but Jackson's campaign was a symbol of how far we've already come. Given the current pace of life in the U.S., the events of the next twenty years promise to be just as complex, fast-paced, and unexpected.

There was still another concern: It is hazardous to generalize about the South. There are so many regional differences. Charleston is not Mobile. Atlanta is not Biloxi. Russellville is not Aberdeen or Amory.

However, I did not allow these concerns to deter me. I contacted friends in the South—including some members of Glenmary—and asked them for their ideas. Looking at the developments in the South during the last twenty years, I tried to discern which trends would likely influence the next twenty. I decided simply to acknowledge that my generalizations might not fit a particular locality or region.

We need a vision of the future, as difficult as it may be to develop one. The ancient Hebrews thought that approaching the future was much like rowing a boat—one *backed* into it, keeping one's eyes focused, for the most part, on the clarity of the past, with an occasional glance over one's shoulder to peek at the murky future.

Today, however, while we dare not forget the past or ignore its lessons, we must peer more intently into the future. In a complex, fast-paced society, we need a clear sense of where we want to go as a community of faith and how we should use our available, but always scarce, resources in order to get there. We must anticipate new needs, challenges, and obstacles. Rather than merely reacting to the pressure of current events, we must also help *shape* the future by clarifying our vision and priorities.

I will offer reflections about the South and the Church in the South during the next twenty years—with the hope that they will make some contribution to the development of such a vision.

Trends Shaping the "New" South

As I noted earlier, there have been many significant changes in the South during the past two decades. I'll begin by identifying some of the major trends and reflecting on their probable impact upon the future.

Before doing so, I must clarify what I mean when I say "the South." There are many ways of defining the term. It may be limited to the eleven states of the former Confederacy or expanded to include additional states, as the U.S. Census Bureau and Gallup Polls do, for example. In this presentation, I'll follow the lead of Father Bernie Quinn, formerly of the Glenmary Research Center, who uses the term, "the South," to refer to the seven states of Alabama, Georgia, Mississippi, North Carolina, South Carolina, Tennessee, and Virginia.

The reality of the South—and, therefore, its public image - has changed considerably since World War II, especially in the past twenty years. Certain trends are shaping the "new" South and will probably continue to do so. At the same time, certain underlying cultural values have proved to have great staying power and will undoubtedly continue to influence life in the South.

"Sunbelt" Demographics and Economics.

Since 1969, there has been an impressive shift of population from the Northeast and Midwest to the so-called "Sunbelt," the southern half of the country from coast to coast. Its climate and relaxed lifestyle have attracted upwardly mobile younger managers and their families as well as retirees on fixed incomes. It has attracted U.S. businesses and foreign investors with its relatively low taxes, nonunion labor, cooperative government, and lower cost of living. This shift—especially to its urban areas—has led to significant social, economic, and cultural changes in the Sunbelt.

During the last twenty years, the South, as I have defined it, experienced a 28 percent overall increase in population, more than 7.2 million newcomers. During the same period, Illinois grew by only 4 percent, and Pennsylvania by less than 1 percent.

However, the South has not seen the dramatic growth found in other areas of the Sunbelt. During the last twenty years, for example, Texas has seen a 50 percent increase of population, Florida a 79 percent increase, and Arizona a 94 percent increase. Moreover, within the South itself, there is considerable variation in population growth. Alabama and Mississippi enjoyed only an 18 percent increase, while South Carolina experienced a 48% increase and Georgia a 59 percent increase.

In other words, the southern states have not equally benefited from the Sunbelt's attraction. And its boons have affected primarily large urban areas—such as Atlanta and Raleigh-Durham—rather than rural areas. The 1987 per capita income in Mississippi was 24 percent lower, and Alabama's 12 percent lower than the *national* average. The disparity between their per capita income and Florida's is even greater.

What A.J. Cooper, the black mayor of Pritchard, Alabama, said more than ten years ago remains true today: "There is a lot of shade in the Sunbelt." In fact, as the newly published **Encyclopedia of Southern Culture** points out, the South has a "higher proportion of poor than the rest of the nation."

Within the South itself, there has also been internal migration from rural areas to urban centers. In part, this is due to the deflation of land values. Between 1980 and 1987, for example, the average value of an acre of farm land in Mississippi dropped by more than 20 percent, in South Carolina by nearly 12 percent.

During the next twenty years, the shift of population to the Sunbelt—and from rural to urban centers—will probably continue, but at a reduced pace. There are already signs that the population density of some regions is having a serious impact on their natural resources and infrastructure, and there has been a reduction in the number and quality of jobs in some areas. So, the South can probably expect to see a continuing increase in both population and per capita income, but with less dramatic results than other areas.

"Southern" Politics

It has been said that there are three things on which Southerners never agree: religion, politics, and barbecue. I will not wade into the arcane world of barbecue recipes, but I cannot avoid tripping through the minefields of southern-style politics. As Professor Ronald Rapoport has reported, the region used to have a "reputation as the home of demagogues, Dixiecrats, and disfranchisement." During the last twenty years, he has pointed out, "reapportionment, the end of disfranchisement, desegregation, and the decline of the one-party system destroyed the institutional foundations of the old political system."

In this process, the old-guard conservatives—primarily at the county level—lost considerable influence. While southern white common folk lost considerable political ground in the 1960s, black Southerners, by and large, benefited from those turbulent times. Recent elections on the national, state, and local levels have demonstrated that the South is no longer a one-party hegemony.

At the same time, there has not been a wholesale abandonment of traditional southern values. The new power brokers in both parties today are often dedicated, articulate champions of conservative ideologies and values. The white underclass tends to support such candidates, while the black underclass—which is growing in numbers and influence—supports a more liberal agenda. The middle class—which traditionally has advocated improved education, health care, job training, housing, and race relations—may hold the key to the future in many areas of the South. In recent years, they have often sided with the new power brokers. If they continue to do so in the next twenty years, there will be little new relief in sight for the poor of any race.

"Bible Belt" Realities

For the most part religion in the South tends to be somewhat homogeneous; it is evangelical, and normative for life. The evangelical branch of Christianity—especially the Baptists—has deep roots in southern culture, and its impact will undoubtedly continue in the next twenty years and beyond.

Nevertheless, the social changes of the past twenty years have also impacted the evangelical churches. They have been influenced to some extent by urbanization, demographic shifts from the North, new prosperity, racial desegregation, and increasing secularization. At the same time, they continue to hold firm to their four basic convictions about the authority of the Bible, direct access to God, traditional morality, and informal worship.

The South will continue to be heavily influenced by evangelical Christians. This means that belief in God, commitment to Jesus as Lord and Savior, high personal moral standards, wholesome Christian family values, and an inspiring reverence for the Bible will continue to be dominant values in the region. Religion for the overwhelming majority of people in the South will be personal, democratic, affective, congregational, biblical, egalitarian, consultative, and charismatic. These are some of the basic realities of the "Bible Belt" which will continue to have considerable impact upon the Catholic Church in the South.

A Vision of the Church in the South

A vision of the Catholic Church in the South during the next twenty years must take into consideration seven basic facts, each of which, in turn, will influence the Church's ministry.

First, the Church will continue to have *minority status.* The number of Catholics in the South has risen dramatically during the past two decades—by 59 percent or more than 425,000 believers. However, the net increase is only 0.6 percent—from 2.7 percent of the total population in 1969 to 3.3 percent in 1989. In Georgia, the Catholic population rose by 153 percent or 132,500 Catholics, but that represents only a net increase of 1.4 percent—from 2.0 percent to 3.4 percent of the total population of the state.

I know what this minority status means from my personal experience. When I was growing up in Columbia, South Carolina, my sister, my two cousins, and I were the only Catholics in our neighborhood and in the school we attended. While I have pleasant memories of that period in my life, being a Catholic in the South frequently meant having to stand up to be counted. It was important to know what the Catholic Church stood for and why we were different from our neighbors.

As a Southerner, I learned the importance of respecting other churches and promoting ecumenism, while appreciating the unique status of our Church and the special gifts it brings to the South. I can truly say that I intuited what Vatican II ultimately stated authoritatively in its **Decree on Ecumenism**, namely, that the Church of Christ "subsists in the Catholic Church . . . although many elements of sanctification and of truth can be found outside of her visible structure." What Jesus gives his Church through the Holy Spirit is the *fullness* of the elements of grace by which the Church is constituted. And it is from that fullness that we offer our gifts: for example, a great love for the liturgical celebration of the sacraments, especially the Eucharist, an appreciation of the role and importance of ecclesial authority, a deep respect for the contemplative dimension of our community of faith, a sense of belonging to a truly global Church and the communion of saints.

So, southern Catholics—while remaining respectful of religious values, sensitive to the powerful role of the Protestant churches, and ecumenically astute—must never, because of their minority status, be hesitant about their Catholic identity and their communion with the Church universal, or about sharing their specifically Catholic gifts with others.

Second, the Church will continue its *inculturation* into southern society. To proclaim the gospel effectively and carry out the Church's ministry well, Catholics will have to be *fully southern*, as well as *fully Catholic*. This implies affirming the prevailing societal values I mentioned earlier: belief in God, acceptance of Jesus as Lord and Savior, high personal moral standards, wholesome Christian family values, and reverence for the Bible - all of which we hold in common with our Protestant brothers and sisters.

However, the last of these—reverence for the Bible—will require more effort on the part of Catholics than the others. Last October, the Notre Dame Study of Catholic Parish Life reported on its findings in regard to rural and town parishes, as distinguished from urban and suburban communities of faith. Rural and town parishioners—presumably in the South as well as other sections of the country—seem to have a stricter sense of personal morality. At the same time, rural Catholics are less likely—and town Catholics more likely—to read the Bible, alone or with others, or to share their faith with others.

Before the Second Vatican Council, Catholics generally were less familiar with the Bible than evangelical Christians in the South. They relied on the ecclesiastical magisterium to make whatever use of the Bible was needed to provide the scriptural foundation for Catholic doctrine and discipline. While the Council helped Catholics regain a deeper appreciation of the Scriptures, this needs to be realized in concrete ways in the lives of our parishioners—especially those in the South, if the Church is to be truly southern.

Third, the Church in the South will carry out its primary mission of *evangelization*. This has many implications. It means re-evangelizing its own members, calling them to accept God's Word into their lives and to change the way they live so their daily activities, attitudes, and values will be in accord with the Gospel. It also means extending a hand of welcome to newcomers, especially Hispanic, Vietnamese, and northern Catholics who emigrate to the South. The Church also reaches out to the unchurched and the black community in its evangelization efforts. And as it reaches out, it must keep in mind the specific needs and cultural values and expressions of these diverse groups.

The Church is faithful to its mission—Jesus' own mission—when it proclaims the Gospel and challenges prevailing cultural values that are not in accord with the Good News. This takes on specific importance in the United States, given the prevailing consumerism, materialism, and secularism which characterize our society—and impact southern culture as well.

Fourth, the Church in the South will make even greater efforts to see that it uses its available resources wisely and effectively. Good *stewardship* of personnel, property, and finances will continue to be a major challenge for Catholics in the South.

As I noted earlier, the number of Catholics in the South increased by 59 percent between 1969 and 1989—more than doubling in Georgia and North Carolina. To accommodate this growing community, many new parishes have been established—226 in the last twenty years, some of them formerly missions. The total number of priests in the South has also increased in the last two decades—but only by 9 percent. Moreover, the number of priests who are retired, ill, or working outside their respective dioceses has doubled in the same period. This means that, in the past twenty years, there has been a net increase of *17* priests in the

South—which also had a net increase of 425,486 Catholics!

The current priest-per-Catholic ratio is about 45 percent higher now than it was twenty years ago. While the overall rate is still much lower than in the Archdiocese of Chicago, for example, priests in the South cover a vastly greater geographical area. Another indicator of this significant trend—more Catholics, increasingly fewer active priests—is the increasing number of southern parishes without a resident pastor: from a total of 8 in 1969 to 81 in 1989. Many of these are served by a priest from another parish, but a growing number are served by a male or female, or a lay person. A few simply remain vacant.

Just as significant is the fact that the total number of diocesan seminarians in the South has plummeted by two-thirds in the last two decades—from 469 in 1969 to 157 in 1989. Religious communities, for the most part, have suffered even greater losses.

Wise stewardship of resources is not merely a matter of numbers. It also involves the quality of pastoral leadership in a given setting. **The Notre Dame Study of Catholic Parish Life** has found that rural parishes, in particular, are often unhappy with the pastor sent to them. Frequently, their complaints center around an authoritarian style of leadership and a lack of liturgical expertise. These are serious complaints in these communities which seek spiritual enrichment primarily through the Mass and expect to share responsibility for these small communities of faith.

For Catholics, the Eucharist is the center of ecclesial and personal life. The greatest challenge for the Church in the South between now and 2009—and beyond—will be to ensure that local communities of faith have regular—ideally, weekly—access to the Eucharist and other sacraments. A concomitant challenge will be to ensure that priests are effective presiders at worship. Presiders at worship in the South of the future will have to develop special skills and gifts. I am thinking, for example, that their preaching must be biblically rooted and thoughtfully presented. This is necessary if they are to prepare their people to live in an evangelical environment and if they are to attract other Christians, as well as the unchurched, to Catholic worship. Indeed, this is crucial to the Church everywhere, not only in the South.

At the same time, pastors will have to learn to share responsibility for the parish with women and men religious, permanent deacons, and lay men and women. Admittedly, this requires a different style of leadership than that prevalent thirty or forty years ago, but the new approach is essential today. Moreover, the conciliar understanding of the nature of the Church and the respective roles of the clergy, religious, permanent deacons, and laity will help us make the necessary transition into the future. It will also ensure an effective, wise use of all available resources.

Fifth, the Church in the South will have to rely increasingly upon *lay leadership.* This is not only a pragmatic matter of compensating for the declining number of ordained ministers. It is also in accord with the teaching of the Second Vatican Council—reaffirmed and further developed by the 1987 Synod of Bishops on "The Vocation and Mission of the Laity in the Church and in the World."

Relying more on lay leaders does not imply diminishing the importance of an ordained clergy. It does not absolve a local church from identifying and supporting in its midst vocations to the priesthood and religious life. The Eucharist and the sacraments are central to the life and ministry of the Catholic Church. And only priests and bishops may preside at the Eucharist in our churches.

Lay people, however, have many critically important roles in the Church—in addition to fulfilling their responsibility of taking Gospel values into their homes, the marketplace, and their communities. The ecclesial needs may differ in rural, town, suburban, and urban parishes, but one thing is common to all: No local church will be able to ignore the need for qualified lay ministers. Fortunately, many dioceses have already prepared lay men and women for a variety of ministries and services.

Sixth, preparing and enabling lay people to carry out appropriate ministries and service in the Church depends upon effective *Catholic education*—from its initial stages throughout adulthood. While information about Catholic elementary, secondary, and collegiate education is readily available, adult educational programs are more difficult to trace statistically.

The Church in the United States has long considered it essential to build a firm foundation in the faith among its youth. The Catholic school system is largely responsible for the strength of the Church—and Catholics—throughout this country, including the South.

During the last two decades, certain significant shifts in educational patterns have taken place in the South, as elsewhere, and must be further studied to ascertain their full significance. Here I will only report the shifts and offer some preliminary reflections on them. The full assessment which they deserve needs to be made during the next few years.

The number of Catholic high schools in the South has dropped by nearly one-quarter since 1969, but the total number of students in Catholic high schools fell by only 7 percent. One might expect that the difference would be reflected in CCD programs for teenagers, but there has been no increase in the number of students in these programs. The numbers have remained fairly the same. Are there simply fewer Catholic high school students in the parishes of the South, or are some of them missing Catholic formation and education during these crucial years?

Since 1969, there has been a greater drop in the number of Catholic grade schools and their students—26 percent and 28 percent respectively, or 25,000 students. There has also been a substantial increase in the number of elementary students in CCD programs—up nearly 50 percent, an increase of more than 33,000 students. The reason for the decline in the number of Catholic grade schools is undoubtedly due to rising costs, competitive public and other private schools, and a diminishing sense of the importance of Catholic education in the minds of some parents.

Rising costs depend upon several factors, but one of the most important is the fewer number of priests, brothers, and women religious teaching in southern dioceses. Today there are 69 percent fewer priests teaching, 38 percent fewer brothers, and 73 percent fewer sisters teaching than in 1969. During the same time frame, the number of lay teachers has more than doubled—from more than 2,300 in 1969 to nearly 5,000 today.

This shift is of more than financial interest. While not every priest or religious in the past was adequately equipped to teach at elementary or secondary levels, pastors and people relied upon them to hand on the faith in fidelity to the Church's tradition. In the next twenty years, we will have to rely more upon *lay* teachers to pass on the faith effectively and faithfully, both in Catholic schools and in CCD programs. This, in turn, means that they have to be adequately trained and formed to carry out their responsibility well.

Finally, the Church in the South must continue to work for *social justice* as it seeks to help build up the Kingdom and shape the social order in light of the Gospel. The Catholic Church has invaluable experience and broad resources to be an energetic partner in the movement towards a just society in the South, as elsewhere. This implies, for example, that Catholics will collaborate with evangelical Christians on such shared concerns as opposing abortion, enhancing family life, and working to preserve marriages.

The Church also emphasizes the social dimension of morality as it addresses such regional problems as racism, unfair labor practices, and a prevailing violence. Taking stands on public policy issues and working for social justice in the South will, at times, be countercultural to the dominant cultural paradigm. But if evangelization is going to be effective in the next twenty years, it must be countercultural.

I would like to suggest that the "consistent ethic of life," which I developed and which now forms the basis for the pro-life activities of the National Conference of Catholic Bishops, provides a credible framework in which to plan and implement, in concert with all people of good will—our outreach in the social arena.

I would like to add here a word abut the Catholic Church Extension Society of which I have the honor of being the Chancellor. For eighty-four years, the Society has assisted the home missions of our country, especially the South. As a young priest working in South Carolina, I came to know firsthand what a blessing the Society is. I am happy to report that Extension is as vital and committed as ever, under the leadership of its President, Father Edward Slattery, and his dedicated staff. Because of the generosity of its benefactors, it is now able to allocate more than $11 million to the home missions each year. As its Chancellor, I can assure you that, during the next twenty years, the Society will continue to assist you in every possible way.

My brothers and sisters, there are undoubtedly many other important considerations to take into account in developing a vision of the Church in the South and of the South in the next two decades. I trust that the perspectives I have brought to this symposium are both *realistic* and *challenging.* Both qualities are necessary.

If a vision is not *realistic,* it will frustrate those who try to implement it. Simply trying to implant a northern vision of the Church in southern soil will not work. It won't take root here, except among the Northern transplants who have migrated here. A vision of the Church in the South must face the reality of southern life and culture.

If a vision is not *challenging,* it will have no power to stir people's souls. Simply trying to carry on "business as usual" and allowing significant changes to take place without meeting the new challenges they entail will spell doom, humanly speaking—for the Church in the South. There are great—almost overwhelming—challenges to meet in the next two decades.

I stand before you as someone with great hope for the Church in the future. The Church in the United States, and the Church in the South, in particular—has many wonderful God-given resources with which to shape the future. I am convinced that we have not yet identified all these available resources—including many of our young people who have the talents and gifts needed for the priesthood and religious life and will respond generously to God's call if we help them in their discernment and support them.

Ultimately, our faith depends on more than our solidarity with one another and our God-given gifts and resources. Hope in the future relies upon God's enduring providence and the ongoing guidance of his Spirit. The Church belongs to the risen Lord, and he remains with us—and will abide with us through the next two decades and beyond—until He comes again. He will not abandon us or grow slack in his loving care and solicitude for his Church, even as he challenges us to use wisely and effectively all our gifts to build up the Church in the future—in the South.

II

THE ROLE OF THE GLENMARY HOME MISSIONERS

Frank Ruff

Fr. Frank Ruff sketches the vision of home mission work to reach beyond the Catholic community. Using five categories of ministry (nurture, ecumenism, evangelization, social involvement and concern for world church) he expands the role of the Glenmary parish to include service to the surrounding community plus awareness of the church universal. For the next twenty years the challenge of cross-cultural evangelization remains the major hurdle for making the Catholic community a church in the South and of the South.

Glenmary has been doing home mission work in the rural South and Appalachia for the past 50 years. We have experience. But the Church has changed. Society has changed. The labor pool is different. Protestants are teammates rather than opponents in the Christian struggle against evil. The cultural differences are greater than we realized. We need help to know how to be true to ourselves, to the people of the home missions, and to the larger church.

We are like a Mississippi farmer whose family has been raising cotton for 50 years. He knows how to raise cotton. But the market is changing. Labor is not so plentiful or so cheap. He is no longer so sure of the pesticides he has been using. He wonders why people don't value cotton as much as he does. He needs help to plan for the future.

Glenmary's Vision

When Glenmary began, it was in response to a clear and definite need. Father William Howard Bishop, our founder, did some basic research and identified more than 1,000 counties in the United States without a resident priest. Most of these counties were in the South from Texas to the Atlantic. One-third of the counties in the United States had no resident Catholic minister and probably a fourth had no Catholic presence of any kind. The 1,000 counties he identified would have made a country as large as Mexico with as many people as Canada. They were neglected by our Church and by many of the governmental, economic, and educational systems of our country as well.

Father Bishop's plan, written in 1936, proposed,

"the establishment of a religious society to labor for the conversion of America to the church of Jesus Christ with the same earnestness and determination as foreign missionary societies are laboring for the conversion of the people of foreign lands."

He was not interested in simply serving the scattered Catholics of the South. He was aware that in the past priests, Brothers and Sisters had concentrated on protecting the faith of Catholics and bringing back fallen-aways. He wrote,

"many a noble priest has spent his life in the saddle going from one little group of Catholics to another, saying Mass in homes, vacant stores, small chapels, instructing children, administering the Sacraments, burying the dead . . . They were sent into the wilds to take care of the Catholics who were there conversions were incidental."

The most common job description for church workers was, and often still is, to serve Catholics, no matter how many or how few there were.

Father Bishop respected these workers, but contended that we would not do our best job if we simply cared for Catholics. We had to develop a "widespread, determined and persevering" program to win new conversions. He wrote,

> *"the Church can never rise to its full stature as a spiritual force even in the lives of Catholics themselves until not only priests and bishops, but the rank and file of the faithful come to the realization that we are a missionary church, founded by Christ to preach and teach the Gospel to every creature and to bring all to follow in his steps."*

His understanding of missionary was always one who reached beyond simply serving Catholics.

At first his focus was primarily on convert-making. But in a letter to Glenmary Missioners in 1952, a year before he died, he expanded their job description. He acknowledged that,

> *"we are all at work trying to bring into the church of Christ as many converts as we can ... We know the satisfaction that comes to one who finds, instructs and baptizes neophytes. But on the other hand we may well ask ourselves, is convert making our only duty? The work of making converts is, of course, the missioner's primary object. But I am convinced that side-by-side with the great convert-making purpose there is another objective for us to cherish and to pursue. That objective is to lift up and improve the moral lives of the people around us regardless of their beliefs or lack of beliefs; regardless, even whether they will ever accept the faith or not."*

He always wanted Glenmary Missioners to reach beyond the Catholic community. In this letter he asked his missioners to work both for conversions and for spiritual development. In other writings he directed Glenmary Missioners to evangelize both individuals and structures, but he never encouraged them to retreat to the care of Catholics.

To ensure the missionary thrust of Glenmary, he called for Glenmary to leave a territory when it was developed. He wrote in the original Plan,

> *"as soon as an area allotted by an ordinary to the society is sufficiently developed to be no longer missionary territory, it should be turned over to the diocesan clergy" and Glenmary Missioners "would move on to a new frontier."*

Glenmary Missioners were not to be just pastoral workers or rural church workers, but true missionaries.

What Glenmary Has Done in the Past 50 Years

We have stayed in the rural South and have made it our home. We have lived and worked only in areas where Catholics were less than about 1 percent of the population.

We are currently doing missionary work in 15 dioceses from West Virginia to Texas. And, I am proud of Glenmary Missioners - priests, Brothers and Sisters, and those who minister with us. Despite the difficulties they have stayed in the trenches. They have not put their hand to the plow and turned back, despite the fact that the ground is sometimes rocky and hard. I know that some of you have been inspired by them and their fidelity.

Also, we have continued Father Bishop's voice calling from the cotton fields of the South and the coal fields of Appalachia to the rest of the American Catholic Church. We have continued to remind the American Catholic Church that there is a true missionary need in the United States. We have reminded them that most of Africa is ten times more Catholic than the rural South. And we have rejoiced that many diocesan priests, many priests and Brothers of other religious communities, and many, many Sisters have come into the home missions.

At this point I would like to pay tribute to some of these mission groups - for example, the Missionary Servants of the Most Holy Trinity, both men and women, the Paulists, the Josephites and the Edmundites, the Mission Helpers of the Sacred Heart, Victoryknoll, Franciscans, Dominicans, Oblates of Mary Immaculate, the Society of the Divine Word, and many others. Moreover, many religious communities whose charism is to serve the poor have come into the home missions. In fact, most of the home mission work which has been done in the United States in the past 50 years has not been done by Glenmary but is the result of the dedication of these Sisters, Brothers and priests. Glenmary salutes them and appreciates them.

Five Categories of Missionary Ministry

During the past 50 years, Glenmary has tried to keep tuned to developments in the larger church. As a result, we have identified five categories of missionary ministry. Today we do not turn back a mission parish until it has reached a certain level of development in these five categories. The first is ministry to Catholics, all of the activity that you expect to find in an alive community, including lay leadership in a variety of settings and education with opportunities.

The second category is the seeking of unity with Protestants, members of Christ and fellow disciples of Jesus with us. We are convinced that ecumenism is a necessary component of missionary life. It is not an elective activity for home missioners.

The third category refers to the unchurched. The first category was ministry to Catholics, the second to Protestants, the third to those who are not members of any church. Those of you who work in Appalachia know that in some places there are as many as 75 percent or 80 percent unchurched, while some places in the Deep South have a relatively small percentage. This category of evangelization includes the sharing of faith in Jesus, as well as Christian witness.

The fourth category refers to social justice and solidarity with the poor and the building of the way of God on earth. Again, any true missionary ministry must include this fourth category and no mission parish is considered established and developed if it does not.

The fifth category is concern for the larger church. We are Catholic and therefore not complete without a vital connection to the diocese and beyond.

The Future Challenge

The good news is that we have stayed in the rural home missions close to the people. Glenmary Missioners have stood with the poor and against racial and economic injustice. We have built bridges to Protestant churches. We have touched and been touched by the people of the rural South. And, more good news is that many other missioners have joined the effort.

The bad news is that we do not do cross-cultural evangelization well. We generally feel at home in a small county seat town and relate rather well to a small Catholic congregation which often consists mostly of northern transplants. But we do not know how to reach the native born Appalachian, the indigenous African-American community, or the rural native born white Southerner, let alone the Native Americans or Hispanics. It is a generalization, but it is generally true that our missionary work whether in parishes or other ministry settings, stumbles on the rocks of cross-cultural evangelization.

We recognize that even after all these years, our ability to adapt to the rural South and its culture is limited. Native-born Appalachian people often do not feel at home in our churches. Even when they do join, they drift away rather quickly. The same is true for the African-American who joins our predominately white churches.

In all honesty, we do not feel particularly at home ourselves with some of the religious symbols of the rural South. For example, we are more comfortable with "Glory and Praise" hymns than with country Gospel or Soul Gospel. We do not know the spiritual hungers and dreams of the unchurched. So, we do not know how to express our faith tradition in a language that speaks to those longings. I told you we needed help.

The poor have had a special claim on us, but more often we do *for* the poor rather than *with* the poor. We have had more experience staying in control of ministry than sharing it. We need help.

I believe that we home missioners need a vision of the Catholic Church *in* the South and *of* the South - one that comes to birth from the Southern culture. We need to know how to evangelize cross-culturally. We chose to place this symposium in a rural Kentucky evangelical setting to help us together taste the culture and find God in it. What we can discover together about home missions will also be helpful to the hundreds and hundreds of other home missioners in the rural evangelical South.

One final question for us. The role of Glenmary from the beginning has been to be a voice pointing out the home mission need and asking for a response. The home missions are bigger than Glenmary. In many ways we are rather insignificant. But we can be a voice for those who have no voice in the Catholic Church. A need I want to voice on behalf of those who have no voice is the fact that there are 155 counties in the rural South in which there is still no Catholic presence of any kind - no faith community, no Catholic worship, no Catholic minister. This has been true in most of these counties, since the founding of the country. These counties are larger than the states of Ohio and Indiana combined and larger than all of New England. More than 2 million people live there. How are we, the American Catholic Church, going to respond to them?

III

CATHOLIC EVANGELIZATION IN SOUTHERN WHITE EVANGELICAL CULTURES

Bill J. Leonard

Dr. Bill Leonard surveys the myths and symbols of the South to highlight their importance for supporting religion in the region. By explaining the myths of authority, church, conversion, ministry and ritual he describes the salient features of Evangelical and Pentecostal churches. His final section indicates how the Catholic church can evangelize in the South.

A few years ago I was invited to lecture on Appalachian religion at a conference held at Jenny Wiley State Park, located just off America's only gravel interstate highway, one of my friends says. The conference was for pastors and laity from churches located in the Appalachian region. These people were natives, many of whom had ministered in the area for years. They were all Protestants; most were Southern Baptists. When I finished surveying certain past traditions and future trends I asked if there were any questions. Immediately a middle-aged pastor inquired: "Do you think we can ever go back to having two-week revivals again?"

That question, to which I gave a resounding "no," says a great deal about the present state and future prospects of Appalachian religion. Even the preachers know that something has changed. Satellite dishes, cable television, pickup trucks and interstate highways have come to Appalachia. No longer can the church command community attention for "protracted" periods of time. The two-week revival is gone forever. Modernity, or worldliness if you prefer, is simply too distracting. The little boy was quite correct when he observed: "Grandma, if you ever go to just one circus, you'll never go to prayer meeting again!"

That is not to say that religious life is dead or dying in Appalachia. Indeed, it continues to be a powerful source of cultural and spiritual stability. Nonetheless, few will deny that major changes are underway throughout southern culture in general, and southern Appalachian culture in particular, changes which have significant implications for religion. Cultural transitions which began in the urban South—Atlanta, Charlotte, Greenville over a generation ago are fast descending upon the hills and hollers of Appalachia. The organizers of this conference were perceptive in their decision to schedule a session entitled, "Catholic Evangelization in White Evangelical Cultures." Any serious discussion of southern Appalachian subculture must give some attention to the broader context of southern white culture in general.

This study is divided into three brief segments. The first surveys the relationship between religion and culture in the American South with particular attention to religious identity. The second part examines certain polarities inherent in southern and Appalachian white evangelicalism. The third segment raises various possibilities for Catholic evangelism in the Appalachian region, present and future.

Religion and Culture in the South

The relationship between church and culture is an increasingly important topic for students of American religion. Many turn for definition to Clifford Geertz's now classic work, **The Interpretation of Cultures**, and Geertz's idea that culture "denotes an historically transmitted pattern of meanings embodied in symbols, a system of inherited conceptions expressed in symbolic forms by means of which (persons) communicate, perpetuate, and develop their knowledge about and attitudes toward life."[1] Through culture a people establishes norms for behavior, values, meaning, and other aspects of common life. To paraphrase the Presbyterian preacher Frederick Buechner, culture is "the world into which you are born and the world that is born in you."[2] This belief that cultural patterns are transmitted through symbols or myths is especially important in the study of southern religion. For it is by means of common symbols and myths that diverse regions and religions in the South were united. Through cultural symbols Southerners developed a means for combining the collective data of their existence. Myths were a way of defining the whole identity of the Southern people. The issue, of course, is not whether the details of the myths were entirely factual, but whether they became an effective, and in that sense true, way of defining collective existence. As Mark Shorer suggested, "a myth is a large, controlling image that gives philosophical meaning to the facts of ordinary life; that is, which has organizing value for experience."[3] Through its myths a society gives meaning to the actual empirical events of its history. Those myths thus provide cultural identity and are perpetuated by the culture they help define. The

1. Clifford Geertz, **The Interpretation of Cultures** (New York: Basic Books, Inc., 1973), p.89.

2. Frederick Buechner, **The Sacred Journey**, (San Francisco: Harper & Row, 1982), p. 9.

3. Mark Shorer, "The Necessity for Myth," in Henry A. Murray (ed.) **Myth to Matchmakers** (New York: 1960), p.355 cited in Patrick Gerster and Nicholas Cord, **Myth and Southern History: the Old South** (Chicago: Rand McNally, 1974), p.2.

American South has been one region where myths and symbols have provided a major source of cultural unity and security. Paul Gaston writes, "what does distinguish the South, at least from other parts of the United States, is the degree to which myths have been spawned and the extent to which they have asserted their hegemony over the Southern mind."[4]

What were the great southern myths? They included the idea of a genteel society, erudite and gracious, concern for neighbor, responsibility for public service, strong personal piety, and the relationship between the races—slavery and segregation, separate but equal— blighted racism. What was the Great Southern Myth? Perhaps it was this: The people who lost the war retained the vision. The defeated people, even in defeat, would be more gracious, more resourceful, more communal than their Yankee counterparts could ever be. In the book, **Baptized in Blood, The Religion of the Lost Cause, 1865-1920**, historian Charles R. Wilson shows how southern churches utilized the theme of the Lost Cause, the idealization of the southern heritage even in defeat, to rebuild the South's spiritual and moral identity. In attempting to help a vanquished people overcome their despair church leaders provided a theological explanation for secular and political events. Wilson writes that southern ministers "saw little difference between their religious and cultural values, and they promoted the link by constructing Lost Cause ritualistic forms that celebrated their regional, mythological and theological beliefs."[5] The actual events of defeat were less important than the way in which they became symbols of and for

4. Paul M. Gaston, **The New South Creed: A Study in Southern Mythmaking** (New York: 1970), p. 8, cited in Gerster and cord, Myth and Southern History, p. xv.
5. Charles R. Wilson, **Baptized in Blood, the Religion of the Lost Cause,** 1965-1920 (Athens GA: University of Georgia Press, 1980), p. 11.

southern culture. The relationship between cultural and religious forces in the South is a prominent theme of recent historical studies. In discussing the antebellum South, Donald Mathews suggested that "religion and the American South are fused in our historical imagination in an indelible, but amorphous way."[6] Mathews observed that evangelical religion enabled both blacks and whites to understand their place in southern culture. Each appropriated a religious experience which provided adherents with "a sense of personal esteem and liberty."[7] Mathews insisted that even before the Civil War, southern Protestant religion was closely identified with "social solidarity." Thus church attendance was at once a "religious act" and "a civic responsibility."[8]

Writing in 1942, sociologist Liston Pope contended that southern churches were among the most powerful social forces in continuing a spirit of isolation and "idealizing antebellum civilization."[9] Samuel Hill, Jr., another insightful analyst of Southern culture, suggests that the "religion of the southern people and their culture have been linked by the tightest bonds. That culture, particularly in its moral aspects, could not have survived without a legitimizing impetus provided by religion...For the South to stand its people had to be religious and its churches the purest anywhere."[10] Southern Protestantism, therefore, helped "remythologize" religious and cultural life, creating powerful symbols by which Southerners understood their place in the world. As those myths falter in the face of pluralism and modernity,

6. Donald G. Mathews, **Religion in the Old South** (Chicago: University of Chicago Press, 1977), p. xiii.

7. Ibid., p. xv.

8. Ibid., p. 249.

9. Liston Pope, **Millhands and Preachers** (New Haven: Yale University Press, 1942), p. 34.

10. Samuel S. Hill, Jr., **Religion and the Solid South** (Nashville: Abingdon, 1972), p. 34.

southern Christians again face the challenge of remythologizing religion and culture in the region.

The intricate relationship between church and culture led historian Martin E. Marty to conclude that southern Protestantism represented one of the most "intact" religious subcultures in contemporary America. Intactness meant that a religious group exercised continuity with its past and provided a unifying sense of identity for its constituents in the present.[11] Marty also suggested that Protestantism particularly the Southern Baptist Convention represented the "Catholic church of the South."[12] Protestantism especially certain forms of it was a *de facto* religious establishment which set various agendas which impacted all religious groups in the region. Within the cultural security of southernness was a theological and spiritual solidarity based on "the primacy of experience in religion."[13] Appalachian religion is heir to many of those cultural and religious ideals. Religious life was, and to some extent still is, a primary source of identity for many Appalachian people. It provided a place, a source of security in the face of poverty, disease and the many unpredictable elements of life. In a sense the mountains themselves were a fortress which protected this unity of culture and religion for a surprisingly long time. But it could not endure forever. Ultimately the forces of pluralism and modernity which spread throughout American life had to find their way into southern, Appalachian culture. Changes brought about by economics, education, civil rights legislation, mobility, family life and secular culture have confronted evangelical Protestantism with new

11. Martin E. Marty, "The Protestant Experience and Perspectives," in **American Religious Values and the Future of America** (Philadelphia: Fortress Press, 1978), p. 40.
12. Ibid., p. 46.
13. Ibid., p. 47.

problems, challenging its religious hegemony in the region. As Southerners moved North searching for employment and as Yankees in U-hauls, not uniforms, invaded the Solid South, pluralism was bound to take its toll. The two-week revival is not the only thing the preachers have lost. As social and religious ties become increasingly fragmented, both church and culture confront an expanding identity crisis.

Any effort, Protestant or Catholic, to bring spiritual witness and renewal to the area should begin with some awareness of the cultural and religious transitions occurring in Appalachia. It should also give attention to some of the basic religious symbols, myths, and belief systems which characterize Protestantism in the region. Thus the second segment of this study focuses on the nature of evangelical religion in the southern and Appalachian setting.

Three ''Families'' of Protestants

Mary Lee Daugherty, director of the Appalachian Ministries Education Resource Center based at Berea College, describes three basic "families" of Protestants evident in Appalachia.[14] "Mainline churches" include Episcopalians, United Methodists, Presbyterians, Lutherans, Roman Catholic, UCC and Disciples. They tend to be more denominationally oriented, with seminary trained ministers, liturgical uniformity in worship, reaching persons through the nurturing sacramentalism of the church. They stress overt social action in response to political and cultural concerns.

Evangelical churches include various types of Baptists, Nazarenes, Churches of Christ, Bible churches and other independent, non-denominational, non-charis-

14. Mary Lee Daughtery, "A Typology of Three Streams of Religious Traditions in the Appalachian Region," typescript.

matic groups. These churches may or may not have seminary graduates as ministers. Many of these preachers are bi-vocational. Their worship tends to be less formal and reflects the influence of the revivalistic tradition with Gospel hymns, Bible preaching and altar calls. Some denominational relationships may be evident but local autonomy is primary. Conversion involves both nurture and dramatic experience. Every individual is encouraged to have a "personal experience with Christ for salvation." Social concerns tend toward issues of personal morality, "traditional family values," and certain New Religious/Political agendas. Fundamentalist theology is a powerful influence in these groups.

Pentecostal churches include the Church of God, Cleveland, Tennessee, the Assemblies of God, Fire-Baptized Holiness, and a variety of independent Pentecostal churches. Clergy tend not to be seminary educated. Some congregations have both male and female ministers. Along with conversion is the strong emphasis on the baptism of the Holy Spirit as evidenced in speaking in tongues, healing and other manifestations. Worship is generally spontaneous with preaching, singing and Spirit expressions. Social concerns relate to personal morality. A strong sense of other-worldliness prevails. These groups have their own problems in the battle against modernity in Appalachia.

Polarities

Yet there may be another way of "mapping" the religious life evident in southern Appalachian evangelicalism. This approach is less concerned for specific beliefs of individual groups than for certain broad, controlling "myths" which shape the theological and pragmatic identity of the churches whatever their specific approach to dogma. It is found in examining certain polarities around which belief systems, myths and symbols take shape. These polarities reflect both the unity and the diversity, continuity and discontinuity, evident in southern and Appalachian white Protestantism.

Myth of Authority

First, Appalachian churches struggle with the myth of authority. Authority is an essential element of the orthodoxy which most churches demand. By what authority human and divine does each groups make its claims? As heirs of the Reformation, Appalachian Protestants insisted that Scripture alone was the rule of faith for the church and the individual. Yet they could not agree on the way in which Scripture was to be used. In the quest for authority some claim to be People of the Book (Primitivism) and some claim to be People of the Spirit (Relevance). Some want to have it both ways. Both of these ideas are present throughout the churches and sects of Appalachia. Faced with a pluralistic religious context many groups claim to be the true and/or only church because they are closest to the New Testament church in doctrine and practice. They are People of the Book, reconstituting the church directly from the Holy Scriptures. They define the church as a community which observes most precisely the practices of the New Testament community. To be the church is to do what the early Christians did. Primitive Baptists believe that they are only a step away from the New Testament church, that their doctrines and ideas are simply a reflection of the earliest Christian church. All other groups promote "man-made" dogmas which are outside the bounds of biblical Christianity. Likewise, persons in the Church of Christ, one segment of the Campbellite tradition, believe that they have restored the Christian church exactly as it was in the New Testament. Through simple faith, immersion baptism "for the remission of sins," weekly communion and no creed but Christ, they claim to have rescued the New Testament church from sectarian corruption.

The question of origins is extremely important to many Appalachian religionists. For example, many Baptists in the region believe that they can trace their lineage by delineating certain Gospel "landmarks" preserved by crypto-baptist congregations since the first century. This trail of blood and martyrs, largely outside of and in conflict with the Catholic church, can be traced all the way back to John the Baptist, immersing Jesus in the River Jordan. This is a form of Baptist successionism ordered, not through bishops, but through local congregations of religious dissenters. Early Baptists in the region sang their theology clearly in this hymn:

Not at the Jordan River, but in that flowing stream,
stood John the Baptist preacher when he baptized Him.
John was a Baptist preacher, when he baptized the Lamb,
So Jesus was a Baptist, and thus the Baptists came.[15]

The so-called snake or serpent handlers carry literalistic primitivism to its logical conclusions, insisting that their practices validate biblical Christianity. "If we don't do it (handle serpents)," one preacher says, "God will raise up a people that will do it."[16] Snakehandler or not, many religious Appalachians view themselves as Bible-believing Christians, often in contrast to other groups who by implication are Bible-denying.

The problem with New Testament primitivism, however, is that the New Testament church was itself quite

15. William Warren Sweet, **Religion in the Development of American Culture** (New York: Charles Scribner's Sons, 1952), p. 158.
16. Eleanor Dickinson and Barbara Benziger, **Revival!**, (New York: Harper & Row, 1974) p. 128.

pluralistic. Which New Testament church, therefore, shall be the model, the churches in Acts, in Paul's epistles, or in the later pastoral letters? Primitivism generally involves selective proof-texting. It also means that many Appalachians may move through a variety of religious groups depending on which seems the most "biblical" at a particular time.

Other Appalachians verify the truth of their doctrine and practice by its relevance, by the activity of the Holy Spirit in the present. They are People of the Spirit, guided, not by arcane "tradition," but by immediate inspiration. The People of the Spirit are the true church, responding as boldly and uniquely to contemporary culture as the ancient Christians responded to theirs, building on valued traditions while discarding or adapting those which inhibited the Spirit's activity in the new age.

Many so-called mainline Protestant groups in Appalachia reflect this idea, concerned that the church not only believe like the primitive Christians but act like them as well, responding directly to the poor and the broken while addressing the social structures which oppress and manipulate Appalachian people. In ordaining women to ministry many of the mainline denominations affirm the guidance of the Holy Spirit beyond the strictures of old literalism.

Pentecostals, on the other hand, claim to have it all. They claim primitivism aplenty, a conformity to the apostolic experience of Pentecost and the book of Acts. Yet the Spirit which spoke at Pentecost speaks yet, through them. This dual alignment of Primitivism and Relevance, Book and Spirit, has made Pentecostalism a force to be reckoned with among the literalistic evangelical churches of the region.

Non-Pentecostals often declare that the charismatic

gifts died with the apostolic age and therefore denounce the spirit people as unbiblical. Pentecostals respond that they simply carry biblical inerrancy to its logical conclusion. The events of the Bible can yet be experienced in these "latter days."

The myth of authority is an important issue in southern and Appalachian evangelicalism today. In diverse ways both modernity and Pentecostalism have raised significant questions about the nature of authority for the church, the society and the individual. Those who wish to minister in the region must give serious attention to the debate over biblical inerrancy and spiritual baptism.

Myth of Church

Another polarity evident in the religious life of Appalachia involves the myth of the church. In this myth the Appalachian churches were pure churches, faithful to the New Testament norm, and, unlike Northern churches, untainted by modernism, liberalism, and worldliness. The quest for purity compounded the tension between the church as People of God and the church as God's Only People. As People of God they were called to cooperation and unity. As God's Only People they were given to diversity and division, competition and elitism.

Unity has long been elusive for the fragmented churches of Appalachia. Sectarian tendencies made many groups hesitant to acknowledge that other churches and denominations were also part of the body of Christ. Cooperation and fellowship between churches, if it existed at all has often been informal and localized. Churches have found occasion for cooperation in various moral crusades in response to social and moral problems and needs. Opposition to liquor sales, lotteries, abortion, and other issues have led to cooperative actions from the churches. Community revival meetings have also provided opportunities for joint cooperation. More recently, community worship services have drawn churches together for common prayer and praise. Ecumenism has been best expressed informally, often selectively, throughout the region. Benevolence endeavors, food pantries and clothes closets also give some evidence of unified ministry and witness as the whole people of God.

Such unity has been relatively limited, however. Indeed, Appalachian Protestants have more often tended to identify their particular group as God's Only People in competition with others for orthodoxy and constituency. Many churches, seeking voluntary membership, competed by claiming to be the only true church, or at least the truest of the true. How better to secure constituents than to convince them that God has only one people and you are it. For many Appalachian religious groups evangelism not only involved winning secular sinners to faith, but proselytizing religious sinners away from false religion. In fact, the more sectarian the group the less likely it is to concede salvation to those outside its fortress of orthodoxy. For years Presbyterians debated Methodists over election and falling from grace. Presbyterians and Methodists challenged Baptists over infant baptism. Campbellites debated everybody. Catholicism represented a fertile mission field for many southern Protestants who readily acknowledged that Catholics were "lost" and that they were often more difficult to convert since they had received Romanist indoctrination from childhood. Today, the sentiment remains prevalent in the region though it is perhaps more subtle. The old doctrinal debates between denominations have shifted to internal confrontations over the nature of orthodoxy within the denominations themselves. Inerrantist Methodists and Baptists, for example, may find greater theological compatibility with each other than with non-inerrantists in their own denominations. Pentecostal Protestants and Catholics now share a common bond which separates them from non-pentecostals in their specific traditions. The idea of the church as God's Only People continues to characterize large segments of Appalachian religion. The boundaries have simply been readjusted. In today's churches, the litmus test may not be the five points of Calvinism but the five points of Fundamentalism instead.

Defining or redefining the nature of the church and the relationship among the churches is an important task for those who would minister in Appalachia in the future. As Protestants lose their establishment status and experience financial and numerical declines, they may find a more practical if not theological rationale for cooperation than ever before. Churches, Protestant and Catholic, may find it increasingly necessary to unite in response to the growing secularism in the region.

Myth of Conversion

A third polarity evident in the Appalachian evangelicalism involves the myth of conversion. Appalachian Protestants are primarily conversionists in their theology of salvation. Eschewing distinctions between the visible and invisible church, they insist that every individual must have a personal experience with Jesus Christ in order to be "saved" from sin and prepared for heaven. The primary purpose of the church of Jesus Christ is evangelism, telling the story of Jesus and snatching souls from the burning. This evangelical imperative involves a tension between conversion as radical event and conversion as nurturing experience.

Heirs of the frontier revivalistic tradition, most Appalachian evangelicals sound as if radical conversion is the only acceptable way of entry into Christ's church. Preachers call for immediate conversion as persons follow the "plan of salvation" to trust Christ and receive new life. Believers new and old "testify to their own morphology (process) of conversion, detailing their transformation from a life of sin into 'new creations' in Christ Jesus." The process of conversion in most Appalachian churches—primitive Baptists are an exception—has been shortened considerably from the often laborious, agonizing process characteristic of early Calvinism to the instant, immediate event promoted by an Arminianized mass revivalism, a kind of "Jesus did it, come and get it" salvation. Sinners are encouraged to pray a simple "sinner's prayer" by which grace is instantly secured and salvation assured. Entrance into the kingdom of God is easier than opening a charge account at Sears.

At the same time, however, Appalachian evangelicals raise their children in the nurturing atmosphere of the church, teaching them from the earliest age that Jesus loves them and that they are welcome in the community of faith. Thus many persons who "grow up in church" testify that their conversion is less a dramatic turning from wickedness and evil than a quiet acceptance of God's love. Many confess that they "never knew a time when they did not love God and believe in Jesus."

Likewise, many Appalachian communions insist on baptizing children very early in life. This often demands some rather fancy theological footwork from those who insist on conversion as a radical spiritual and moral crisis. Baptists, for example, rejected infant baptism but worried that children might pass the "age of accountability," that mythic time when the child became morally responsible and therefore deserving of damnation. Since no one could be sure when that occurred, the imperative for baptizing children increased considerably. Often these children testified, not to a dramatic conversion from sin, but to a willing response to the Christian nurture they had experienced in community of faith. When they encountered adolescence and adulthood, and really sinned, many feared that their earlier conversion was invalid. Some repudiated their childhood experience for a newer, more dramatic experience of grace, one in which they "understood" what they were doing. This process reflects a type of infant/child baptism followed by confirmation. Thus conversionist churches allowed for nurtured but also required dramatic conversion as a means of finding full acceptance in the community of faith.

The myth of conversion and its accompanying theology of evangelism is in disarray among many of the southern and Appalachian churches. It deserves serious attention by all those who seek to minister in the region.

Myth of Ministry

A fourth polarity in Appalachian religion involves the myth of the ministry, the nature of leadership in the church. It involves the age-old tension between the priesthood of all believers and the authority of the preachers. In one sense, Appalachian churches claim to be "people's churches," founded on a rabid egalitarianism in which all the saved are ministers, witnessing for Christ, carrying the Gospel to the world. Many mistrust denominational alignments as detrimental to the autonomy of the local congregation and the liberty of the individual believer. Many congregations exist only unto themselves, denouncing hierarchies and institutional alignments as unbiblical. Salvation thus becomes the great equalizer by which social, economic and spiritual superiority is abolished. Faith is not mediated from clergy or institutions but comes directly from God to the individual. Whatever ordination may exist in the church is the result of a divine mandate, not the approval of some ecclesiastical body. Authority comes from the Holy Spirit working in the life of the lone believer or congregation. Even those churches that do affiliate with denominations wear their denominational loyalty loosely.

At the same time, ministerial authority in Appalachian churches remains a powerful force to be reckoned with. Preachers, ordained or otherwise anointed, maintain an important position as mediators of the word of God and leaders of the church. In many religious traditions in the region, the "call to preach" is the most exalted vocation in the world. Fundamentalist churches, for example, place great emphasis on the authority of the pastor in the divine "chain of command," the divine order of things. The pastor is the "undershepherd," who is directly responsible to God for the souls of his flock. In these churches ministry and maleness are inseparable, again a part of the divine order. The faithful are admonished, in the words of Scripture, to "touch not God's anointed," or in other words, "don't mess with God's man!" Likewise, the minister's place in the divine order is closely related to the husband as head of the house and the subordinate role of women in the family and the church. In many Pentecostal churches, however, such distinctions are less arbitrary. The Spirit moves where it will and may fall on women as readily as men, particularly in the "latter days."

Tensions between the people and the preachers occur with considerable regularity in Appalachian churches. Conflicts over ministerial authority create splits in churches which in turn creates new churches. Sometimes the preachers leave, taking their supporters with them.

Sometimes they remain and a dissonant group goes elsewhere. Likewise, self-proclaimed preachers appear throughout the region founding their own churches and starting their own ministries. Denominationally based churches debate the effectiveness of a seminary trained preacher over a non-seminary preacher. The increasing numbers of women pursuing vocation in pastoral ministry, even in Appalachia, promises to be a significant issue for the churches in the immediate future.

Myth of Religious Ritual

One final issue deserves attention. It involves the myth of religious ritual. On the surface, many Appalachian churches appear to be adamantly opposed to "ritualism" in their approach to worship and the sacramental. Their concern is for that spontaneity of the Spirit which has no place for written prayers, sermon manuscripts, and "corpse cold liturgy." They denounce ritualism as unbiblical, detrimental to heart religion and dangerously "Catholic." Ritualism is a sign of the decline of the church and genuine faith. True churches are not ritualistic. In their fear of ritual, many evangelical groups so devalued traditional Christian sacraments as to leave them almost devoid of meaning. Many Baptist preachers, for example, assured their congregations that baptism and the Lord's Supper were "only symbols," activities which Jesus had ordered ("ordinanced") and which the obedient New Testament church would obey. Baptism and communion were observances "tacked on" to the preaching service, hurriedly carried out with little sense of divine presence. In many Appalachian churches parishioners are "symbol starved," looking for ways to discover transcendence and mystery.

At the same time, Appalachian churches cultivated certain rituals which nurtured a sense of the sacramental. In very basic ways, numerous churches established simple but profound observances for baptism, communion, foot washing, anointing with oil and other observances, creating some powerful new rituals which provided the people with visual and symbolic expressions of personal and communal faith. Perhaps the best example of this is the invitation or altar call. In many evangelical churches and revival meetings, worship services conclude with an invitation to conversion and Christian commitment. Persons are urged to "come forward" to accept Christ, join the church or "surrender for full-time Christian service." In many ways, the invitation became the evangelical sacrament, an outward and visible sign of an inward and spiritual grace. In fact, in many Appalachian congregations the invitation replaced baptism as public confession of faith. Converts described their conversion in the language of the invitation: "when I came forward," "when I walked the aisle," "when I shook the preacher's hand." Indeed, many testified that conversion itself took place in the very movement from pew to aisle. Thus the people who claimed to be non-ritualistic, or non-sacramental, created and renewed their own symbols, sacraments and signs by which they acted out dramatic moments of faith.

Catholic Evangelization in the South

That leads to a final segment of this study, the question of strategies, methods and goals for Catholic evangelization in the Appalachian region. In response to that endeavor I would like to provide some analysis of the state of religion in Appalachia and then discuss some ways in which Catholics might respond perhaps as agents of "remythologization."

What is the state of religion in Appalachia? I would suggest that it is a time when the old myths, the old ways of identifying faith, are increasingly unstable, if not in serious disarray. First, one of the most serious problems involves the nature and method of evangelism. While some churches and denominations in the region have moved away from 19th century revivalistic methods, many seem uncertain as to what kind of evangelism should be developed to replace it. Those communions which retain revivalistic methodology seem equally confused regarding the meaning of evangelism itself. Many promote what might be called an evangelical transactionalism by which salvation is simply a matter of assenting to certain ideas, praying and completing a transaction by which salvation is forever secured, no muss, no fuss. As H. Richard Niebuhr noted long ago, conversion has been institutionalized in such a way that, "Regeneration, the dying to the self and the rising to new life—now so apparently sudden, now so slow and painful, so confused, so real, so mixed—becomes conversion which takes place on Sunday morning during the singing of the last hymn or twice a year when the revival preacher comes to town. There is still reality in it for some converts but, following a prescribed pattern for the most part in its inception and progress, the life has gone out of it."[17]

Many Appalachian evangelicals are forced to recognize—however grudgingly—that the old revivalistic methods are increasingly less appealing. I believe that this is one reason for the drastic rise in "reconversion" and "rebaptisms" among Southern Baptist church members and the emphasis on such reconversion by professional evangelists. Indeed, one popular bit of humor suggests that some Georgia Baptists have been immersed so frequently that they remain perpetually wrinkled! Rather than confront the theological and practical im-

17. Richard Niebuhr, **The Kingdom of God in America** (New York: Harper Torchbooks, 1973), pp. 179-180.

plications of a faltering theology of evangelism, many preacher-evangelists preserve statistics and orthodoxy by converting the already converted, often wreaking spiritual havoc for the sake of statistical success. Evangelism needs serious study and reevaluation in Appalachian churches.

Second, fundamentalism is setting an agenda for many of the churches in Appalachia, a fact which cannot be overlooked or underestimated. The Reagan Era, the rise and fall of various television preachers, and the activities of fundamentalists in denominations and local churches worked to make people, fundamentalist dogmas and movements a significant force in America in general and the South in particular. Fundamentalism is supplying preachers and churches with a theological system for understanding faith, worship, politics and life itself. It defines the nature of Scripture and doctrine, citizenship and salvation for a growing number of persons. Religious groups outside fundamentalism must not hesitate to develop strategies for responding to the fundamentalist system. This need not take the form of attacks on fundamentalists or their particular ideology, but involves a willingness to develop alternatives which respond to the same needs but in different ways. Like it or not, fundamentalism has set an agenda for religion in Appalachia. It cannot be ignored or underestimated. For example, fundamentalism defines the nature of Scripture—inerrantist; the nature of faith—transactional-rightwing; the nature of America—chosen, Protestant nation; and the nature of the church—conformity. What alternative biblical, doctrinal, personal and communal theologies can be developed?

Third, Appalachian religion is experiencing confusion regarding the nature of the church. Old denominational alignments no longer command the loyalty they once did. Denominational programs and ministries are experiencing serious financial difficulties. Likewise, local congregations confront divisions regarding finances, ministerial authority and theological orientation. Is the church primarily an agency of salvation, bringing persons to salvation and training them in a life of discipleship? Is it to respond to public issues of personal and corporate morality? Should it "win people to Jesus" and take mine owners to court? In an increasingly secular environment, what ministry will it provide for those who do not accept its Gospel of grace but who need care nonetheless?

With those questions in mind, we now turn to the issue of Catholic evangelism in the region. With fear and trembling this Protestant, evangelical, non-fundamentalist Southern Baptist makes the following observations and proposals.

First, I would suggest that Catholic evangelism in Appalachia begins with presence and service. Presence means a willingness to go into the region, to new areas and to be with the people. This means being with Catholic people and non-Catholic people alike. It is a willingness to incarnate a witness in service to all persons. Service, therefore, is the place to begin. Given the legacy of anti-Catholicism in the region, immediate acceptance as a viable religious alternative may not be possible. Persons will be drawn primarily by Catholic service—no questions asked—to the pressing needs of the people. There is already evidence of that in various Catholic ministries in the region, particularly those of religious women.

Second, Catholic evangelism in Appalachia must be unabashedly biblical in its public expression. Bible preaching, Bible teaching, Bible witness are essential. Old caricatures that Catholics "don't believe the Bible" die hard in the region, even among those who do not necessarily attend any church.

Third, Catholic liturgy must reflect a blend of the sacramental and the pietistic. Heart religion nurtured on powerful symbols of the church can be an important element in worship and evangelism. As we have said, many persons long for evidence of the transcendent and the sacramental in their lives. They can be drawn to faith as they find that aspect of faith cultivated in the community of faith. This seems to me a great strength of Catholicism these days. In a sense, Protestant evangelicalism and Roman Catholicism are passing like ships in the night, moving the opposite directions. Fundamentalist Protestants seem obsessed with ministerial authority while Catholics are reasserting the ministry of the laity in new ways. Lay participation in worship is essential in Appalachia.

Finally, Catholics must participate in the renewal of a theology of evangelism in the church. Indeed, I would hope that Protestants and Catholics would find ways of doing that together. The most serious question facing the church in America, I believe regards the nature of evangelism in the 21st century. No longer can we take our cues from 19th century evangelicalism or sacramentalism. But in moving away from old methods we must not give up evangelism entirely. Likewise, Catholics and mainline Protestants must not allow the term "evangelical" to be used by only one segment of Christ's church. All Christian communions are evangelical, all are witnesses to the good news.

Perhaps Catholics in Appalachia might work to remythologize conversion, moving beyond certain 19th century modes toward a more ancient form—evangelism by and into community. This would take seriously the importance of individual decision within the communal stability of the church. It would acknowledge that to be saved is to belong to a people, the communion of saints. Churches might therefore reassert a theology of evangelism grounded, not in rabid individualism, but in union with a people, the People of God.

IV

EVANGELIZING HISPANICS IN THE SOUTH

Yolanda Tarango, C.C.V.I.

Sr. Yolanda Tarango affirms the authentic contribution of popular religion among Hispanic Catholics. This maintained their faith even when the institutional church ignored them. Family values, critical to understanding Hispanic people, preserve the culture with its deep religious roots. The story of Our Lady of Guadalupe offers a message that expressed good news for the indigenous Indian culture by promoting dignity and respect for the future direction of evangelization among Hispanics.

The characteristic that best describes Catholic Hispanics in the South is invisibility. This invisibility is evidenced by the lack of resources about this group and the lack of social and political influence experienced by the group.

The majority of Hispanics in the rural South are of Mexican origin, though there is an increasing number of Central Americans swelling the population. Many are migrant farmworkers or arrived in the South as migrant farmworkers. The majority feel alienated and powerless in society's institutions and in the churches, though the Catholic religion does provide an important point of unity for the Hispanic family. If I were to sub-title this presentation, I would call it *Familia y Fe.* Family and Faith.

The Hispanic community in the United States is characterized by a deep rootedness in faith and a strong family oriented religious tradition which has been nourished primarily by the women.[1] These characteristics have been the two major sources of strength and continuity for Hispanics. In their pastoral letter on Hispanics, the United States Catholic Bishops correctly state:

In many respects the survival of faith among Hispanics seems little less than a miracle. Even at times when the institutional church could not be present to them, their family-oriented tradition of faith provided a momentum and dynamism accounting for faith's preservation. But let us not depend only on that tradition today; every generation of every culture stands in need of being evangelized. (EN, 54)[2]

This statement by the bishops captures several of the elements I would like to address in this presentation. In the first place, there is the recognition of the faith and faithfulness that characterizes Hispanics in spite of years of neglect and misunderstanding by the institutional church. There is also acknowledgement of the role of the family in faith's preservation. These two elements must be taken into account before addressing the topic of evangelization of Hispanics in the United States. The "seeds of faith" residing in the Hispanic community have been nourished and have yielded abundant fruit. This does not mean that the work of evangelization is complete, however. As the bishops further state, we cannot depend only on that tradition today, we must continue evangelizing every generation.[3] Therein lies the challenge before us.

---

1. **A Pastoral Letter of the Hispanic Bishops**. The Bishops Speak With the Virgin. December, 1981. p. 8.
2. National Conference of Catholic Bishops. **The Hispanic Presence: Challenge and Commitment**. December, 1983. #9.
3. Ibid.

As I venture further into the topic of evangelization and Hispanics, I would like to be as clear as possible about the scope of this presentation. I hope to come to a deeper understanding of evangelization as the essential mission of the church[4] and of the implications for carrying out this mission among Hispanics in the United States today. The title, **Evangelizing Hispanics in the South**, can be interpreted to suggest a "how to" approach that packaged for a homogenous group. It should be understood I do not intend to offer such a formula for evangelization nor to homogenize the cultural aspects of Hispanics.

Defining Hispanics

Hispanic people live throughout the United States and can be found in every diocese of the Catholic Church in this country. In some areas we are the majority of the Catholic population. As Hispanics we share a cultural legacy different from that of indigenous North Americans, North Americans of African descent, and those of Anglo-Saxon or other European descent. We share a common language, Spanish, but we reflect a multi-faceted diversity. We may be brown, or black, or white, reflecting the blending of blood and culture which we proudly claim as our mestizo[5] heritage. We may be bilingual or monolingual in either Spanish or English. Our cultural histories and myths are different as are the reasons we live in this country.

Mexican-Americans living mainly in the Southwest, are the largest group of Hispanics in the United States.

4. Pope Paul VI. **On Evangelization in the Modern World**. December, 1975. #14.

5. Mestizo: "half-breed," "hybrid." Used here to describe the mixing of Spanish, Black and Indigenous blood to produce a new people. For a longer discussion see: Virgil Elizondo, **Galilean Journey: The Mexican American Promise** (New York: Orbis Books, 1983).

We are also the group that has been here the longest. Many of us consider ourselves indigenous to the Southwest and have a profound identification with the land. We necessarily take offense when referred to as immigrants and will often point out that the border crossed us; we did not cross the border. In my own experience, my family has lived on the same land, one mile from the present United States-Mexico border, for many generations.

The sense of being indigenous to this part of the country is also exhibited in the attitude of Mexicans who migrate to the north for a better life. The border is an abstraction to them, after all, the United States Southwest was the northern half of Mexico.

Another group that is primarily, though not exclusively, of Mexican origin is the migrant farmworkers. These seasonal workers over the years have been responsible for spreading the Hispanic presence across the country. As they travel in three major migrant streams they often settle in places along the way and attract others, thus forming Hispanic communities, often in the most remote areas of the country. It is this group that comprises the majority of Hispanics who live in the rural South.

Puerto Ricans and Cubans form the next largest numerically indentifiable groups of Hispanics. They both share Caribbean culture and a blending of Spanish, Indigenous and Black heritage. Puerto Ricans are U.S. citizens since 1917, though they have been coming to the continent in migrations since 1910. Their pattern of migration is cyclical as they move between the continent and the island on a fairly regular basis. Puerto Ricans can be found in every state but are concentrated primarily in the Northeast and industrial midwest. Cubans have come to this country in three major waves since the early

1960s. The first exodus began in 1959 when Fidel Castro rose to power. Between 1965 and 1973 another group of Cubans came as part of the "Freedom Flights." This exodus came to a standstill until 1980 when the Port of Mariel was opened and another large group of Cubans arrived in the United States. The largest convergence of Cubans is in Florida and moving up the east coast of the country.

To add to the diversity, there are Hispanics from Spain, South America and Caribbean countries such as the Dominican Republic. The largest influx of Hispanics presently, however, is from Central America. In the midst of all this diversity the majority of us share a deep Catholic faith. It is this faith which has been at the root of our struggle against assimilation and loss of our language and traditions. It is in fact, the explicit expression of this faith that has helped us to maintain our culture.

Hispanics Neglected

In the bishops' pastoral letter on Hispanics, "The Hispanic Presence," the authors make reference to the survival of the faith among Hispanics as "little less than a miracle." This statement is an allusion to the unresponsiveness of the official church to Hispanics for many years. For many of those years few Hispanics had a voice in speaking to our own concerns within the church. Over the past fifteen years an increasing number of Hispanic leaders have presented our concerns before bishops, religious orders and national Catholic conferences. As I prepared this paper I reread some of those presentations as well as the conclusions of the Primer, Segundo and Tercer Encuentros, and the National Pastoral Plan for Hispanic Ministry. I realized that we are speaking with a unified voice, and that that voice has not really been

heard. We are still re-echoing the same issues and recommendations that we presented fifteen years ago:
- Evangelization incarnated in our cultural context
- Greater respect and understanding of the role of popular religion
- Increased opportunities for lay and female leadership
- Development of small ecclesial communities
- Promotion of apostolic movements as effective instruments of evangelization
- Ministry to the family in order to support its evangelizing efforts with the youth
- Participation in the structure of the church
- Integration not assimilation

We must ask ourselves why the Hispanic voice has not been heard. In part, the neglect we have experienced as Hispanics has been due to historical circumstances, but also to xenophobia. Fear of the foreign seems to be a characteristic not only of United States society, but of the churches in this coutnry, to the degree that they have uncritically assumed the culture. The Catholic Church, in its own process of struggling against the perception of being foreign and its desire to succeed in the American context, became assimilated. It also became an agent of assimilation, by promoting "Americanization." It is in this role that many Hispanics have come to know the Catholic Church in the United States. The result has been cultural distance between Hispanics and the official Church, which translates into a lack of trust and a feeling of being outside of this institution. In other words, many Hispanics view the Catholic Church in the United States as a primarily Anglo institution, and associate the degree

6. Hurtado, Juan. **An Attitudinal Study of Social Distance Between the Mexican American and the Church**. Mexican American Cultural Center, 1976. (p. 44-46)

of belonging to the Church with the degree of assimilation into the dominant United States culture.[6]

When will society and our church fully accept us as first-class citizens? When will our church permit more use of our language and culture in the Mass without fearing that the Church's unity will be destroyed? When will the church in the United States cast its lot with the poor and alienated? When will society and the church admit not only in theory but also in practice that it is all right to be different? These are voices of Hispanics who feel neglected and who feel that at times the church has been more interested in "Americanizing" than in evangelizing its people.[7]

Additional factors which have contributed to the neglect of Hispanics in the institutional church include the fact that Hispanics coming to this country have usually not been accompanied by native clergy. In the case of the Southwest, the native clergy who were already present were ousted by the French bishops, who assumed the leadership after the territory came under United States jurisdiction. The development of indigenous Hispanic leadership, on the other hand, has been virtually impossible because of the racist structures in seminaries, convents and educational centers. This situation has left the area of pastoral ministry in the Hispanic context open to foreign clergy who often have not understood or valued the community's traditions. These same clergy have rarely spoken the language of the people.

Other factors that have impeded the proclamation of the Good News in the Hispanic context are the imposition of a foreign model of evangelization and the disregard of popular religion. The mainstream model of

7. From a paper presented by Father Frank Ponce on "Hispanics and the Church." National Conference of the Catholic Bishops, Spring, 1980.

evangelization promoted in the United States Catholic Church is almost in direct opposition to the traditional model Hispanics have experienced. Popular religion, which has been a sustaining structure of religious expression for Hispanics has generally been ignored or combatted by the pastoral agents of official religion.[8]

These factors are neither new nor all-encompassing. Yet, they are important for understanding the impact that they have on the present and future process of evangelization among Hispanic people. For example, I believe further reflection on the contrast between the mainstream and Hispanic models of evangelization as well as on the strong hold of popular religoius practice, would add insight to the present topic. Further, I believe these offer a key to the future involvement of Hispanics in the United States Catholic Church.

Evangelization Among Hispanics

The methodology of evangelization, the way religion is taught and faith is communicated, can vary according to the different circumstances of culture and values of the group.[9] The methodology in the mainstream model is linear and individualistic. The emphasis has been on personal relationship with God, individual conversion and knowledge of the Church's laws and teachings. The evangelized person is one who "knows" about their religion, and presumably, acts on it. Conversely, the system in which most Hispanics have experienced evangelization is circular one where religion is taught through feeling and example. Stories, rituals and symbols are employed to communicate religious values. Transmission from parent to child is spontaneous and

8. Deck, Allan Figueroa, S.J. **The Second Wave**. Paulist Press, 1989. p. 57.
9. Pope Paul VI. **On Evangelization in the Modern World**. December, 1975. #40.
10. Deck, Allan Figueroa, S.J., **The Second Wave**. Paulist Press, 1989. p. 57.

natural.[10] The evangelized person "feels" close to God and this motivates his or her life.

My faith and my involvement with the Church is because I *siento* (feel deeply) that it is part of my life, not because I follow many of the church's rules...[11]

When confronted with persons evangelized in this model the assessment from the dominant perspective may be that they do not give evidence of "knowing" much about religion. The mistake is in considering such people unevangelized. Yet, that is precisely the conclusion that has often been drawn. The result has been evangelization programs aimed at increasing knowledge. Worse, these evangelization methods do not take into account the person's experience and understanding of faith. What we have to strive for is a sense of continuity, a methodology that begins by respecting and validating the individual's faith experience and building from there. Therefore, when speaking of evangelization among Hispanics we must first be concerned with the "way" of knowing. The content will be revealed in the process. For example, during interviews with Hispanic women about their religious experiences, the following were some of their responses:

I resemble my parents because they had a lot of faith. It was not a faith based on the church, it came from within them; it was part of their culture, part of their life.[12]

My grandmother was a very religious woman. In the family she was the epitome of faith, the epitome of religion. And that was so not only in my family but in the community - that is still true. My first memory of praying is of going with my grandmother to visit people

11. Isasi-Diaz, Ada and Tarango, Yolanda. **Hispanic Women: Prophetic Voice in the Church**. Harper and Row, 1988. (p.18).
12. Ibid, p.18.
13. Ibid, 28.

in the community. She helped others, went to be with others.[13]

I do not remember my father praying like my mother did, but he is a very nonverbal person and his faith is very much linked to who he is and the work he does. My father was a laborer and was very proud of that. He always told us, "When you fill out the applications, be sure that you write that I am an unskilled laborer." He felt honored by what he did. He would borrow a car - we did not have one - and he would tell us, "Look, I am going to take you to see all the buildings your father has made." Now, as an adult, I have learned that the virtue that best describes my father is meekness.[14]

My grandparents were the ones who set an example for me when I was young. In a very special way I have to mention an uncle of mine. He was never married; he was blind in one eye and saw just a little out of the other. In the house my mother had an altar, my grandmother had an altar...and when this uncle would wake up, the first thing he would do was pray...The example of my grandmother, my mother, this uncle gave me was of having faith in God; they always hoped that one day it would be better for us. Maybe they would not see those better times, but the younger ones would.[15]

In these statements, Hispanic women are talking about their understanding of the faith, particularly as embodied in the spirituality of their families. They speak about God, not in abstract concepts, but with examples of faith-filled people. Faith, understood in this framework, is not acquired through knowledge but is an interior "knowing" rooted in a person's total being and communicated by example. Faith prompts service, gives dignity and meaning to life and encourages hope for a

14. Ibid, p.29.
15. Ibid, p. 40.

better future. The "way" of knowing then, is not through intellectual knowledge but through experience. Three essential and constitutive dimensions of the Christian faith are 1) faith as believing, 2) faith as trusting, and 3) faith as doing.[16] All of these elements are evident in the statements of the Hispanic women quoted above. If the church, then, is to "deepen, consolidate, nourish and make ever more mature the faith of those who are already called the faithful or believers,"[17] it must begin by recognizing and respecting the long faith tradition embodied in the community. While faith is a gift from God and its growth is a gift of the Spirit, it is the church, in the case of Hispanics - the domestic church - that has nourished it.

On the other hand, programs that aim at "educating" us, are often patronizing and alienating. They begin with the assumption that the person lacks certain knowledge. When directed at the Hispanic community they are often designed to relate to "simple" people with inherited faith but no understanding. This approach to evangelization is not acceptable in the Hispanic community. It reinforces in us the sense of being outsiders in the church. In order to belong, it seems we must receive a certain body of knowledge and tradition. Yet, there is no indication that our faith experience will become part of that tradition.

Our challenge to the church's evangelizing efforts then, is that it begin with the assumption that we are evangelized. This does not mean that we are merely the inheritors of a simple and childlike faith, but rather, that we bear a long and mature tradition. We want the church to help us to nourish and deepen our understanding of

16. Groome, Thomas. **Christian Religious Education**. Harper and Row, 1980. p. 57.
17. Pope Paul VI. **On Evangelization in the Modern World**. December, 1975. #54.

this faith, through a process that promotes continuity with our cultural experience. We want to be part of the church, not only at the receiving end, as persons to be evangelized, but as evangelizers. We also want the church in the United States to reflect our contribution to the faith tradition in this country. This means that our religious practices and customs would be accepted as appropriate, not only for ourselves, but for the entire Church. By the year 2000, it is estimated that Hispanics will comprise half of the United States Catholic Church. This reality will require a new way of understanding and describing the Catholic Church in the United States.

Any consideration of evangelization among Hispanics in the United States must necessarily take into account popular religion. The importance of this form of religious expression among the people requires us to give it serious consideration. Popular religion has provided the form and structure for maintaining cultural identity, as well as for keeping religious experience alive in the Hispanic community. The historical circumstances of Hispanics in the United States have been a contributing factor to the growth and development of popular religious practice. Neglect in the Church and isolation in the society left Hispanics feeling marginalized and abandoned. This experience did not lessen religious fervor. Instead, it nurtured the formation of a family based religion.

Expressions of popular religion include traditional devotions such as the rosary, novenas, Way of the Cross and processions. Others include culturally distinct activities, such as Posadas during Advent and Quinceaneras, to mark a significant passage in life. There is an entire calendar that encompasses the religious and liturgical celebrations of the Hispanic community. In addition, there are the symbols and practices that are part of daily home life such as the *altarcitos* (home altars), devotions to special saints and mother's blessings before leaving home each day and at bedtime. The people often feel more "bound" by the rites of popular religion than by those of official Catholicism. For example, they would be less likely to interrupt a novena than to miss Mass on Sunday. Centuries of Catholicism have not abolished some practices - they have merely removed them from the Church premises. There are many examples of devotions, ousted from the parish church, that have taken up residence in someone's home. Some rituals hold the power of sacraments, such as Ash Wednesday. Few Hispanics would lose the opportunity of receiving ashes on this day. Holy Week is also a very meaningful time, calling for identification with the sufferings of Jesus. Its importance even takes precedence over Easter Sunday. Holy Week is especially significant for its Christological emphasis. It is the only time, apart from Christmas, that popular piety focuses on Jesus. Consequently, Hispanics who have been strongly influenced by popular religion do not have a strong Christology. Their understanding of Jesus is more influenced by tradition and popular practices than by the Gospel. The emphasis of popular piety is on God, Mary and the saints. The only other time Jesus is central is at Christmas when the stress is on the "Baby" Jesus.

As I stated earlier, popular religion has provided the framework for maintaining the language and traditions of our ancestors. It should be respected for its power within the community rather than seen as a threat to official Catholicism. The Document on Evangelization in the Modern World recommends, "Above all one must be sensitive to it, know how to perceive its interior dimensions and undeniable values,...When it is well oriented,

18. Ibid. #48.

this popular religiosity can be more and more for multitudes of our people a true encounter with God in Jesus Christ."[18]

Thus far I have taken a cursory look at how neglect, xenophobia and the absence of indigenous leadership have robbed the Gospel message of some of its energy in the Hispanic community. I have also contrasted the mainstream and Hispanic methods of evangelization in order to point out the alienating potential of the normative approach and to indicate the starting point for ongoing evangelization efforts. I have also spoken of our desire as Hispanics to have the official Church recognize our evangelization and to work with us to deepen our understanding of this faith in ways that are respectful of our experience and culturally sensitive. In order to do this our experience must be understood so that the ongoing process of nourishing our faith can have continuity. We also need to understand and respect the role of popular religion.

The Role of Family Life

I would like to look now at how we continue to evangelize succeeding generations of Hispanics in the United States, particularly in the rural context of the South. The task takes on new dimensions as we look at the weakening of the Hispanic family in the United States cultural environment. This weakening is due to the considerable forces of assimilation as well as to the social and economic pressures created by a technological society. The *Segundo Encuentro*, in 1977, singled out the family as needing special pastoral attention.

Priority should be given to the Hispanic family, because it faces increasing disintegration due to a tech-

19. **Proceedings of the II Encuentro Nacional Hispano de Pastoral.** **August, 1977. p. 72.**

nological society, materialistic values, and economic and cultural problems which threaten it and with which it must contend.[19]

The call, by the participants at the Segundo Encuentro, for primary attention to the family is based on the recognition of this institution's role as a primary agent of evangelization. We affirm that the structure of the church ought to serve the evangelization and the liberating salvation of the whole person...We especially single out and support the fundamental value of the family in the world and in the church...we propose: That the Church urgently analyze and commit itself more to the human and Christian growth of the family, because the future and hope of the Church resides in the family, which is the one that forms our youth.[20]

Traditionally the family has played a critical role in evangelizing generations of Hispanics. To some extent this task was aided by the neglect and isolation experienced by Hispanics in the religious and social context of the United States. The Hispanic community's response was to insulate itself with its own language, traditions and religious practices. Thus, both cultural and religious survival were assured. Hispanic children, however, had to adjust to living in two worlds. We interacted with the educational system and the official Church, then we came back to the world of the family. It was understood that we needed what the dominant culture could teach us in order to survive in the society, but the world we trusted was that of the home.

Very early on I separated the religion of my home from what the church taught me. The priests in my church were Spaniards, but what they said was not the real thing for me. The world of prayer at the house was

20. Ibid, p. 68.
21. Isasi-Dias, Ada and Tarango, Yolanda. **Hispanic Women: Prophetic Voice in the Church**, p. 29.

separated from the church. It was very frustrating for me as a little girl because I went to church and heard what they said, and then I had inside the other me.[21]

In this statement it is evident that the "home religion" held the greater power. As Hispanics become less isolated, and more vulnerable to assimilation, the Hispanic family is confronted by increasing intracultural differences between parents and children. This conflict is shifting authority outside of the home. Interaction with institutions of society, as well as the desire to become integrated into that society has caused many Hispanics to put more credibility outside of the family. Some manifestations of this are: loss of the Spanish language, lessening of popular religious practice, and low cultural identity. Additionally, the economic environment has forced more women into the workforce and further weakened the transmission of culture and values. The result of all of this is that the Hispanic family today is struggling to remain a vital force in the evangelization of succeeding generations.

This struggle of the Hispanic family to remain a credible agent of culture and evangelization is being experienced in the rural areas as well, though perhaps at a slower pace. Hispanics living in rural areas continue to experience greater isolation and, therefore, to depend on the extended family structure to insulate them from a hostile environment. Their lack of economic resources, generally low educational achievement, and often a language barrier, causes them to feel alienated from most of society's institutions, including the church. Consequently, one of the primary characteristics of Hispanics living in the South is their invisibility and marginal presence in both society and the church. This is consistent with what has been identified as the main characteristic values of rural Catholic Hispanics:

1) Devotion to Catholicism, to traditional expressions of faith
2) Closer relationships with family neighbors
3) Respect for elders.[22]

The Hispanic model of evangelization described earlier has a much stronger hold in the rural than in the urban areas. However, the family is still losing influence in the evangelization of younger generations. As the young Hispanics interact with society's institutions, the clash between traditional and modern views becomes evident.

The weakening of the Hispanic family in the United States and its lessening influence in communicating traditional values does not eliminate its possiblity as an evangelizer. It would be naive to expect that this method of evangelization would remain constant in the midst of tremendous social change. The role of the family remains significant, but it needs more support from the institutional church and its pastoral agents.

The evangelization of the present generation of Hispanics must have two points of departure.[23] It must be rooted in the traditional values that have shaped our identity as Catholic and as Hispanic. It must also be based in the experience of the United States culture in which we live. Therefore, the challenge to evangelization today calls for a critical understanding of the present cultural milieu and a knowledgeable respect of (for) our Hispanic religious roots. Effective evangelization in the Hispanic community will require support of the family and creative continuity of the rituals and symbols that have expressed Hispanic faith for many generations.

The Message of Guadalupe

22. Nira, Teresa. "The Rural Catholic Hispanic," **Rural Roots**, May/June, 1986.
23. Deck, Allan Figueroa, SJ. **The Second Wave**. Paulist Press, 1989. p. 116.

The primary symbol of Hispanic evangelization is captured in the image of Guadalupe. One cannot speak of evangelization among Hispanics without speaking of Guadalupe/Tonantzin. This is our founding myth as Christians. In the Guadalupe story we find a bridge of continuity between the past and the present, a message that radically expresses good news by promoting human dignity, and a methodology that is effective because it is inculturated among those who most need good news, the dispossessed. The story of Guadalupe/Tonantzin encountering Juan Diego is filled with the religious-cultural imagery of the people. The encounter occurs at the pilgrimage site of Tonantzin, the Mother Goddess of the Aztecs. The woman appears, surrounded by the signs and symbols of the people, and incarnated in their likeness. Thus, she affirms the basic dignity of the people, recognizing their past, and, through her request that a church be built, inviting them to participate in the future. This event occurred in 1531, just ten years after the conquest, at a time when the people felt that they too had died after witnessing the destruction of the world they knew.

The person of Juan Diego and the way the woman relates to him are also indicative of an approach to evangelization. She addresses him as "Juantzin, Juan Diegotzin." The *tzin* suffix is a title of honor, signifying reverence and respect. By addressing Juan Diego in this way she recognizes his worth, thus counteracting the message of a society that says he has no worth. When Juan Diego protests, asking her to send someone of higher status to carry her message to the bishop, she reminds him that he is her chosen one because he who is worthy of respect has been reduced. The message, like that of the Magnificat, is that God restores the position of those who have been brought down.

The approach to evangelization that the Guadalupe story suggests is one which is concerned first with promoting dignity and justice among those who have been wronged. "It is when the Gospel makes 'somebody' out of the 'nobodies' of society, when it restores the self-worth of the marginated, when it enables the oppressed to have a reason for hope, when it empowers the poor to struggle and suffer for liberation and peace,"[24] that it is the good news that the people need to hear.

24. Costas, Orlando e. "Evangelism frm the Periphery: The Universality of Galilee," **Apuntes**, Winter, 1982.

V

CATHOLIC EVANGELIZATION AMONG SOUTHERN BLACK PEOPLES

Jamie T. Phelps, O.P.

Referring directly to the teachings of **Evangelii Nuntiandi,** *Sr. Jamie Phelps handles the basic theory of evangelization by emphasizing personal and social transformation. This involves salvation and liberation in both the historical and transcendent realms. Effective evangelization requires the use of methods and symbols suitable to a specific time, place and culture. Citing Josephite Father John Slattery of the nineteenth century as an example, Sr. Jamie encourages a holistic evangelization with black Catholics participating in decision making for liturgical inculturation and the transformation of oppressive social and political structures in the North and South.*

In the following pages, I will outline a basic theory of evangelization and its method. I will examine the Josephite Mission among southern blacks in the nineteenth century in light of this theory, and suggest some implications of this theory and history for contemporary evangelization of black people in the South.

Basic Theory of Evangelization

1.) Meaning and Purpose of Evangelization Personal and Social Transformation

We must begin with defining the meaning and purpose of evangelization. According to **Evangelii Nun-**

tiandi, evangelization is the process of "bringing Good News into all the strata of humankind and through its influence transforming humanity from within and making it new..." This "new humanity" emerges as the newly baptized (or the "re-evangelized") begin to live lives according to the Gospel. The purpose of evangelization is the "interior change...of the personal and collective consciousness of people, the activities in which they engage, and the lives and concrete milieux which are theirs." (**EN** #18)[1]

> . . . Through the power of the Gospel, [hu]mankind's criteria of judgment, determining the values, points of interest, lines of thought, sources of inspiration and models of life which are in contrast with the Word of God and plan of salvation [are upset and affected]. (**EN** #19)

2) Evangelization Involves Witness and Explicit Proclamation

Evangelization involves, therefore, the transformation of individuals and cultures by the twofold method of witness to the implicit proclamation of the Good News internalized and manifested by ones' behavior; and by explicit proclamation and acceptance of the Gospel into the life of the individual and the community. This acceptance of the Gospel is manifested most initially by the entrance of those moved by the Gospel into a community, called church, as a sign of one's genuine commitment and intention of becoming active participants in the mission of the church. (**EN** # 21, 22, 23).

3) Evangelization is Theocentric and Christocentric

Evangelization is God-centered (theocentric). It is the Good News which bears witness to God manifested

---

1. **Evangelii Nuntiandi** #18.

in creation, in the life of Jesus Christ the redeemer and in the power of the Spirit who makes all things new. Its central message is Christ-centered (Christocentric): evangelization announces God's desire for the universal salvation of humankind as evidenced by the redemptive act of Jesus Christ through whom "salvation is offered to all as a gift of God's grace and mercy." (**EN** #26, 27).

4) Evangelization Involves Salvation and Liberation Understood as Historical and Transcendent

This salvation involves historical and transcendent elements. Salvation involves human advancement, development and liberation as well as the hope of future participation of humankind in the reign of God ushered in by the power of the Holy Spirit. Salvation is therefore existential, i.e., "this worldly" and eschatological, i.e., "other worldly." Salvation involves justice, i.e. action on behalf of social reform of the oppressive forces and structures in society and the permanent union of humankind with God and with one another in God. Salvation is liberation! Liberation of the Gospel involves liberation from the concrete and historic forces of oppression as well as the liberation of humanity to the realization of its openness to the divine absolute i.e. God. Liberation necessitates conversion of hearts as well as transformation of oppressive systems and structures. (**EN** 30-33)

Inculturation of the Gospel

Effective evangelization requires the use of methods and symbols which are suitable to specific time, place and culture. In other words, the Gospel must be inculturated. One must interpret the central messages of Jesus Christ found in the Scripture and Church teachings in a manner which evokes a dynamic response of hope which grounds one's motives for living lives conformed to the patterns of right-relationship modelled by Jesus during his earthly life. Members of a particular culture must have their life experience affirmed, challenged and transformed by the Gospel. Marcel Dumais has compared these three moments of inculturation to the central events in the life of Christ, the Incarnation (acceptance); Death (challenge) and Resurrection (transformation).[2] Those aspects of a culture which are consistent with Gospel values (life, love, justice, living in accord with the will of God) are affirmed. Those aspects of a culture which lie in contradiction to the Gospel (customs, systems and patterns of relationship which threaten the life of some of the members of the community) which deny God's universal love and perpetrate injustice (dehumanization, unemployment, homelessness, miseducation) must be challenged. Such challenge results in a change or transformation of the culture and its individual members.

The Josephite Mission of John Slattery: A Case Example

Although the Mill Hill Fathers began their mission to the emancipated slaves in John R. Slattery, who would become known as the prime mover of "Negro" evangelization in the late nineteenth century, Slattery did not begin his ministry on behalf of blacks until 1878 and his direct involvement in evangelization until 1884 in Richmond, Virginia. Slattery's introduction to the principle of inculturation were rooted in his reading the writings and corresponding with Charles M.A. Lavigerie, founder of the White Fathers of Africa. Lavigerie wrote of the

2. Dumais, Marcel.

necessity of the adapting to the life style and customs of those one was seeking to proclaim the Good News:

> *We must assume as much as possible the manner of the natives, we must speak their language, wear their garments, eat their food, in conformity to the example of the apostles: 'Become all things to all men, that we may save all.'*[3]

Slattery sought to replicate the model of holistic black education he discovered at Tuskegee in his visits and conversations with Booker T. Washington and his visits to Hampton Institute. Slattery's attempts to use inculturated methods and his observation of the effectiveness of black Protestant clergy eventually led to our understanding the absolute necessity of a "native clergy and catechists" to incarnate the Gospel among blacks.

To date, I have not uncovered data to ascertain whether Slattery's inculturation attempts included his understanding of and interpretation of the Scripture. However, his acceptance of blacks as human beings having the same "universal call to salvation" and his understanding of the "universal brotherhood of men" based on their common creation, redemption and empowerment by the Father, Son and Spirit, led him to challenge some of the social and ecclesial conventions the nation and church.

The Post-Reconstruction was a period of intense hostility to blacks. No longer viewed by the North as a political asset nor seen by the South as an economic necessity, black life was characterized by exploitation, disenfranchisement, contempt, discrimination, segregation and lynching at the hands of white individuals and white institutions. The African-American community was marginalized from the social and political activities of the major political parties and its educational needs

3. Phelps, Jamie T., "John R. Slattery's Missionary Strategies," **U.S. Catholic Historian**, p. 212.

were being increasingly met by the emerging black church-related or private industrial schools. Blacks developed independent farms, small businesses, and labor unions and self-help groups..[4]

Slattery associated with black social leaders and established training institutions which sought to educate black and whites for the evangelization of blacks. His understanding of evangelization was holistic. He understood that the preaching of the Good News included fostering a spiritual relationship of blacks with God as well as struggling to educate and train blacks to function in the broader society and participate in the evangelization of other African-Americans. Within the racist context of the nineteenth century, Slattery was met by opposition in these endeavors from whites who still maintained the moral and intellectual inferiority of blacks as a rational explanation of their exclusion from the social, political and ecclesial positions of power and responsibility. A poignant example of such an attitude is found in a letter written in September 22, 1900 by a Nannie B. Younger. Younger has decided to discontinue her subscription fund raising for Slattery because of his new policy of training Negroes for the priesthood:

I am sorry not to help you in the education of priests, and if I had it, would give a great deal, but I must confess, the Cardinal notwithstanding to the contrary, I would a great deal more, to keep the Negro out of the priesthood. It is said to take three generations to make a gentleman, and I am sure it will take unnumbered generations of the most favorable circumstances, to fit the Negro to be a decent Catholic. No foreigner not even the people of the North know the Negro like we do, and I will regret with all my heart ever to see one ordained, we have scandals now but it would [be] infinitely worse with Negro priests. Protestants have great respect for the priesthood now, but put the Negro

4. Phelps, Jamie T., "The Missionary Ecclesiology of John R. Slattery: A Study of An African-American Mission of the Roman Catholic Church in the Nineteenth Century." Catholic University of America, 1989: (unpublished dissertation).

in it, and they will naturally conclude it is not much, and I would not blame them for thinking so...I am not prejudice against the Negro and no one has more kindly feeling toward him, but I am as sensitive to the honor of the Church and the dignity of the priesthood, as I can be, and would dislike more than I can tell, to hear of one being in it...[5]

Younger's attitude of the superiority of whites in contrast to the moral and intellectual inferiority of blacks was characteristic of her times and was held not only by southern clergy, religious and lay white Catholics, but by Catholics from the North as well. Slattery's eventual withdrawal from the church was partly influenced by criticisms of his work from other priests and the indifference of the Church to the evangelization of the Negro.

Slattery had a holistic understanding of evangelization which led him to develop institutions for the moral and educational development of the African-Americans as well as institutions to provide for black priests and catechists who could participate in the effective inculturation of the Gospel in the African-American community. Commitment of his efforts to the evangelization of the oppressed blacks led to his isolation and hostility toward the Church which he saw as generally indifferent to the evangelization of blacks in a nation whose enmity for black life was manifest by social and political marginalization and hostility expressed by undereducation and lynching.[6]

The Current Context

More than one hundred years later, the vast majority of African-Americans in the North and South are the

5. Younger to Slattery, September 22, 1900, JFA: 16-R-10.
6. "Missionary Ecclesiology," Chapter 1.

victims of continued institutional and interpersonal racism within the society and the church.[7]

While a small minority of African-Americans enjoy economic stability and some participation in the social and political fabric of the general society, the vast majority live life in poverty and face the daily negative realities of hunger, inadequate housing, unemployment, poor education, family disintegration, imprisonment, black on black crime, poor health care, and high infant mortality rates.

In the North with the flight of whites and upper middle class blacks to the suburbs or gentrified core of the central city, poor blacks remain isolated in neighborhoods experiencing economic depression and abandonment by life support services, such as hospitals, adequate food stores, banks, etc. In the South the rise of middle class blacks to social and political privilege is minor in comparison to the continued massive poverty of rural southern areas. Some areas of the South have the advantage of a more stabilized extended family.

The Catholic churches in both North and South follow patterns of segregation. In the North, these patterns were established by white flight: in the South they are the remnant and sign of the continued racism which is at the core of black-white relationships. Beneath the veneer of the New South is the old attitudes of white superiority and black inferiority. In the North and South the vast majority of black Catholic churches are staffed by white priests and religious. Some of these have engaged in constructive reorganization of their parishes to involve participation of blacks in policy making, decision making and have patterns of liturgical inculturation. Many have continued patterns of paternalism and maternalism which reinforce the perspective

7. "Brothers and Sisters To Us," Washington, D.C., USCC, 1979.

African-American inferiority. Evangelization is low key at best, while maintenance of traditional parish and limited renewal occupy the majority of the attentions of the parishes.

Many black Catholic churches in the South, like their sister churches in the North are struggling for survival. While some maintain large congregations, these typically are conservative and manifest few signs of inculturation or proclamation of the concrete historical liberative aspect of evangelization which call for the transformation of social, political and ecclesial structures which continue to oppress and dehumanize blacks.

While some blacks participate in the social, political and ecclesial structures of the South, this participation is usually limited by the authority of the whites who tend to hold the power positions in the government and churches. Only in those churches or institutions where blacks are totally in charge is participation more inclusive, and even many of these restrict planning and decision making for effective evangelization, and social action to the pastor and his pastoral associates alone. Often these pastors are cross-cultural ministers who have failed to listen or adapt their approaches to the particular needs of the parish or region in which they are ministering. As a consequence the Good News is not heard in an inculturated fashion, and the parish remains small and isolated from the community. Blacks in some areas of the South think of the Catholic Church as a totally white institution.

While Church mission in the South varies from state to state and region to region, often the social justice mission of the Church is treated as a totally disparate aspect of evangelization. The parish churches engage in "spiritual uplift" and charity, while groups like the Catholic Committee of the South join with the social and political struggle for justice led by non-church related organizations.

The Challenge

The Catholic Church in the South, like that in the North, must be challenged to engage in a more active effort at holistic evangelization whereby black Catholics are allowed to participate in the planning and decision making of the internal affairs of the parish and to the organize within and through the church for the change of those social and political structures which inhibit the nurturance and sustaining of black life. Many black Catholics remain unaware of the social justice teachings of the Church and their call to exercise their baptismal responsibility to participate in the spiritual and social-political transformation of society. While one's commitment to the Gospel mandates a deep personal relationship to God, it also mandates a commitment to social justice. **Evangelii Nuntiandi** teaches that evangelization entails the proclamation, witness and formation of community based on the Good News of the Reign of God, the central message of Jesus' proclamation which promises a liberating salvation, liberation "from everything that oppresses man [and woman] but which is above all liberation from sin..." (**EN** 9) This is good news for African-Americans whose lives are characteristically restricted and threatened by racism.

VI

EVANGELIZING ROLE OF THE CATHOLIC LAITY IN THE HOME MISSIONS

Joe Holland

Joe Holland creatively employs the metaphor of addiciton and codependency to describe the destructive forces within society and the church. The church enables a deadly anti-ecological addiction in Western culture by its misplaced emphasis in spirituality. The healing and future re-evangelization of society requres a non-clerical spirituality rooted in the laity.

In looking forward to the next twenty years, I propose that there are only two scenarios available to Glenmary, a pessimistic one and an optimistic one. Normally futurists propose a third in-between scenario, but because of our present crisis I do not think Glenmary has the choice to be mediocre. Your only two choices, I propose, are (in the words of Black Catholic evangelist James Goode) to flourish or to perish.. I propose that either you will become the servants of a new and dramatic Catholic evangelization in the home missions, or that as a congregation you will die.

The reason for these stark choices are twofold. First, we are living amidst a fundamental crisis of white Western culture, a crisis whose depths are revealed by the twin afflictions of the ecological poisoning of our earth and its personal echo in our youth, the poisoning of their bodies through drugs. Both afflictions, in my view intimately related, form part of a great death wish in Western civilization.

Second, we are living amidst a fundamental crisis of Catholicism in the areas of white Western culture, at least in Western Europe and North America. In the second half of the last century, large areas of Western Europe were spiritually devastated by a massive process of Catholic de-evangelization, as if a spiritual atomic bomb had been dropped on Europe. In the second half of this century, I believe we are beginning a similar process of Catholic de-evangelization for the United States, and perhaps for all of North America.

Some might say we in the West live amidst a dying culture and a dying church. Not to be so dramatic, I would prefer to say we live amidst a declining culture and a declining church. In this context of at least social and Catholic decline, there is no room for mediocrity. Either we will succumb to the decline, or we will find fresh new spiritual energy for a dramatic renewal of our faith and our culture.

I have been asked to speak with you today about the laity and evangelization in the home missions, all in relation to Glenmary's future over the next twenty years. In developing this theme in relation to our present context of social and religious crisis, I will:

First, review some *new insights in regard to addiction and codependency*—insights which offer us a liberating way to understand our present crisis of church and society;

Second, sketch the *addictive crisis of modern Western culture* and how Catholicism has been secretly complicit in that addiction, in turn precipitating the current institutional decline of Catholicism in Western culture;

Third, propose that a precondition of the healing of our culture and its Catholic re-evangelization is *rerooting our spirituality power in the laity*, and that this rerooting can guide Glenmary opening's to the laity in the evangelization of the home missions during the next twenty years.

To understand the lay challenge for the future of evangelization in our home missions, it is necessary first to understand the evangelical challenge of our presently difficult situation, namely that Western culture is in a serious addictive crisis, and that within that crisis Western Catholicism is in serious institutional decline. But to understand this claim, I begin with a review of the metaphor of addiction.

A. THE METAPHOR OF ADDICTION

Presumably you are familiar with the experience of addiction—be it to the abuse of alcohol, drugs, sex, work, power, approval, or whatever.

I use the metaphor of addiction not to scapegoat addicts, but for two reasons outside of obvious addicts themselves. First, the enslavement of addiction and the liberating struggle against it serve as windows into the dynamics of sin and grace among all of us. Second, addictions and the struggle against them occur not only within individuals but also within institutions, including the church.

Addictions are a metaphor for sin, for the pathological decision through a deepening habit not to choose life, but rather death. The addiction itself is a pseudo-religious ritual, a compulsive evil communion with the suppression of life. Sin as addiction is an attempt to escape from the risk of the vocation of our own creativity—with each other, with the earth, and with God the ultimate creator. Addiction is a death-dealing flight from this God-given spiritual power, a denial of the image of God within us. Thanks to the work of 12-step programs stemming from Alcoholics

Anonymous, we now have three important pieces of information about how addictions work.

First, the major block to healing any addiction is *denial*. Facing the truth of the addiction is the first step to overcoming it.

Second, addicts are generally supported by what are called *enablers* or codependents, who deny the addiction in others, cover it up, and help to smooth things over. Helping the enabler to face the truth, along with the addict, is key to their mutual recovery.

Third, both these pathologies are fed by a *loss of self-esteem*, that is, a failure to accept that we are made in the image of God. There can be no healing without a recovery of God- given self-esteem.

The Device of Denial

Let us look first at the device of denial. Prior to beginning recovery, the addict always denies that the addiction exists. The logic of that denial is perfectly clear. Only by deceit does sin thrive. As Jesus tells us in the Gospel of John, "Everyone who practices evil hates the light. They do not come near it, for fear their deeds will be exposed." (John 3: 19-20)

The antidote to the lying of addiction is simple the *truth*. The addict and the enabler begin to overcome the addiction only when they face the truth of the addiction's existence, of their own powerlessness before it, and of the need to appeal to a power greater than themselves. That power is God. As Jesus said so simply, ". . . then you will know the truth, and the truth will set you free." (John 8: 32)

Let us turn now to the second lesson about addictions—the mutually destructive alliance of the addict and the enabler or codependent.

The Mutuality of Addictions

We might say that the addict and the enabler are really two different forms of addiction. One is actively aggressive, while the other is passively aggressive. The addict is addicted to a direct habit of physical or psychological violence. The enabler is addicted to an indirect habit of covering up and playing the martyr role.

Traditionally men—as husbands or lovers, fathers or sons—have more often been the addicts, while women—as wives or lovers, mothers or daughters—have more often been the enablers. But in reality both the active addictive and passive enabling temptations are present within all of us. We may be subject to the addict's temptation in certain circumstances and to the enabler's temptation in others.

As we know from the Book of Genesis, the full image of God is found only in the combination of female and male. Thus we read in Genesis 1:27, "God created humanity; in the divine image God created them, male and female God created them." For this reason, the sacrament of marriage is perhaps the richest symbol of God's full face revealed through creation.

In a perverse way, however, the disfiguring of God's image in humanity by the destructive mutuality of active and passive addiction occurs most powerfully through what might be called a negative marriage, that is the destructive cooperation between addict and enabler—again often respectively male and female. The addict and the enabler enter together into a masochistic-sadistic dance of scapegoating and self-pity, repeated over and over with increasing ferocity. Where authentic marriage opens itself to new life, this alliance of addict and enabler ultimately seeks death.

The Loss of the Image of God

The third insight about addiction is that both the addict and the enabler are fed, in different ways, by a loss of self-esteem, or better by a blocking within their consciousness of the creative risk of carrying in themselves the image of God.

The addict is tempted to deny God's image within oneself by putting oneself above God, in effect a macho defiance of the need for any greater power. The addict implicitly pretends to have on one's own and without God the fullness of assertive power and to exercise that power without love.

By contrast the enabler is tempted to deny God's image within oneself in the opposite way. The enabler puts oneself far below God, in effect pleading not to be worthy of being considered in God's image. The enabler claims to exercise love, but in that exercise to be helpless and to have no power at all.

Thus the addict tries to grasp power without love, while the enabler tries to love without power. Both thereby try to avoid the risk of their creativity by mutually denying their responsibility for it. But we are profoundly responsible for the creative life which we have within us from God's own image, and accountable for it.

The Healing of Addictions

The healing for these mutual pathologies comes from just the opposite patterns, namely by so enriching our God-given self-esteem that we dare to accept the risk of our creativity and so accept accountability for it. This happens by becoming increasingly conscious of the loving presence and life-giving power of the image of God within us. But this happens in different ways for addict and enabler.

The addict, or the active aggressive partner, is healed by weakness, that is by a softening of the drive for power. This occurs by accepting that our power can be life-giving only when it is open to receive in love. In this process the feminine face of God within us frees our masculine side from the sinful compulsion to triumph in violently physical or psychological domination over people and things, over whom we are tempted to impose power.

The enabler, or passive aggressive partner, is healed by strength, that is by a toughening of love. This occurs by discovering that love can be life-giving only when it grows out of our own inner power, and does not depend on approval from others. In this process the masculine face of God within us frees our feminine side from the sinful compulsion to depend for meaning on others, to whom we are tempted to grant power over us.

The healing regeneration within ourselves and in all of life comes from the creative communion of these female and male images of God. We either embrace their creative dance thus share in bringing forth new life, or we turn away into a sadistic-masochistic flight toward death.

As Moses told the children of Israel on the banks of the River Jordan, these are ultimately our only two choices—death or life. (Deuteronomy 11:26) And as Jesus told us, those who would try to protect their lives by security will lose life, but those who would abandon security to risk their lives will gain life. (Mark 9:35)

The Link to Evangelization

I have developed this metaphor of addiction and its healing by the fullness of the female and male image of God, as the mutually fertile source of our own creativity, because, as mentioned earlier, social and ecclesial institutions can have their own addictions to active and passive destruction. Leaders and members in these institutions can choose to hide from the risk of their responsibility for creativity by self-deceiving, addictive and enabling patterns of untruth, and thus consign themselves to institutional decline and even death. That, I believe, is the presently destructive threat to our society, to our church, and perhaps to Glenmary as well.

Or we can accept the truth of our own powerlessness over our addictive or enabling patterns and then appeal to God for healing and new life. That, I believe, is the creative alternative for our society, for our church, and perhaps for Glenmary as well. Let us now sketch what might be called the addictive crisis of Western culture and within it the enabling role of Western Catholicism.

B. THE CRISIS OF WESTERN CULTURE

I will focus in this second part of my paper on the addictive nature of our ecological crisis, its anti-spiritual manifestation in sectors of the contemporary youth culture, its relation to misguided dimensions of Western Christian spiritualities, and how these are all linked to the decline of Catholicism in the West. This analysis in turn will provide for us a basis for perceiving the centrality of a lay-rooted re-evangelization of Western culture and for the challenge to Glenmary during the next twenty years for lay evangelizers in rural America.

In this analysis it is important to remember that there are not two worlds, the world of society and the world of the church. No, there is only one world, God's creation. Our Christian story of this creation is a simple story, yet we so easily forget it. First God created the world, and saw that it was good, or we might say "holy." Second, we humans wounded the world by sin. The word "wounded" is important, for though we damaged the world, we did not completely destroy its goodness. Third, in Jesus the healing of the world begins—building on the goodness that is still within the world, yet finding new depth in Him. These three moments then—creation, wounding, and healing—are our simple story. A key part of this wounding its its ecological alienation.

The Addiction of Ecological Destruction

I am deeply indebted to Catholic visionaries like Charlene Spretnak and Thomas Berry for teaching me that the fundamental addiction of our modern urban-industrial Western society is ecological, or rather anti-ecological. From them I have learned that, in the name of human progress, Western culture is addicted to an ever more violent poisoning of our precious planet. This poisoning of our planet is a direct assault on all forms of life on earth, including our own. In the name of improving life, we are in fact killing it.

There are social parallels to this anti-ecological addiction, parallels which have their distinct but linked dynamics, especially the oppressions of racism, sexism, classism, and ageism (including the attack on the unborn). There are also linked and parallel patterns of ideological addiction. But I limit my reflection here to this foundational anti-ecological addiction and its roots in Western Christian spiritualities.

This anti-ecological attack is not unique to Western culture, but can be found seminally in the general rise of high civilizations since the Neolithic age. But the spiritual justification for it was more developed by certain Western Catholic spiritual teachers. And the attack has been dramatically intensified in Western culture since the rise of the modern era, and particularly since the Industrial Revolution. Similarly, the reaction of Catholic spiritual teachers since then has enabled the anti-ecological attack to deepen.

In times past the anti-ecological attack was technologically capable only of inflicting small bruises upon the earth's life system. Today, however, because of the vast power and scale of our advanced industrial technologies, we are now inflicting deadly wounds.

Not long ago, the undersea explorer, Jacques Cousteau, celebrated the 25th anniversary of his work. In a special PBS television program, Cousteau showed some of his first underwater movie photography done 25 years ago in the Mediterranean Sea. The footage revealed colorful underwater plants and exotic fish—images one would associate with Tahiti or the Bahamas.

Next Cousteau showed films of those very same areas of the Mediterranean Sea today. There were no more plants. There were no more fish. The bottom was covered with old automobile tires and pieces of rusting metal. The water was murky. Everything was dead, d-e-a-d, dead.

Finally, Cousteau said, the same process of the death of a sea, which he saw unfolding in the Mediterranean, was presently beginning in the great oceans of the earth. The oceans, of course, are the mother of all life on earth. Without the continued nurturance of the oceans, all life on earth will die. Yet right now, the human family, led by Western culture, is killing the great oceans.

As we all know, the anti-ecological attack is not limited to the oceans. It hits streams, rivers, and lakes, as well as forests, topsoil, air, even the ozone shield above the air, and all the living species. Though there are new signs of ecological renewal, so far these are but faint cries of resistance against an ever growing industrial assault.

Its Manifestation in the Youth Culture

Even if we succeed in reducing the intensity of this violent assault upon the earth, we will still leave a bleak legacy. In the words of Thomas Berry,

It is already determined that our children and our children's children, are going to live amid the ruined infrastructure of the industrial world and amid the ruins of the natural world itself.

The only adequate way, I believe, to understand this deepening poisoning of the earth is through the metaphor of addiction. We, as a culture and even more broadly as a species, are spiritually addicted to poisoning our earth and ourselves. We are compelled to repeat the addictive cycle, dependent institutionally upon its violence, and spiritually powerless before its destruction.

It is especially from youth today that we are forced to face the truth of this addiction. So many of our children now inflict on their own bodies the same violence which we inflict upon our ecosystem. As we pour poisons into the earth, so many of our youth now pour large doses of the poison of drugs and alcohol into their own bodies. Some of these youth are now creating a culture of nihilism and even of satanism, for example through certain strains of heavy metal music.

By so doing, these youth simply repeat and reveal in their own bodies what our wider culture does on a much vaster scale. As our culture seeks ecological death, so their artistic energy reveals and ritualizes the terror of that death. These youth have in effect created a negative religion—complete with its own rituals, chants, ecstasy, and communion of drugs—to internalize the destruction of the earth which daily unfolds in the external world around them.

In creating this negative religion of death, these Western youth also reveal to us the crisis of Western

Christian spiritualities. They would describe Western Christianity as bankrupt, hypocritical, and (worst of all for them) boring. Boredom is of course the result of the loss of creativity. But I would rather describe the state of Western Christianity as part of the anti-ecological addiction—not the active aggressive partner who does the obvious damage, but the passive aggressive partner, the enabler or codependent, who facilitates the addiction by ignoring its presence, covering it up, and trying to make everyone feel good through denial.

Roots in Western Catholic Spiritualities

A culture is fundamentally shaped by the spirituality at its core. For historical reasons too complex to explore here, the spirituality at the core of Western culture became afraid of the disclosure of God in and through the earth and its fertile sexual energy. In particular, Western spirituality became afraid of the immanent disclosure of the feminine face of God, and tried in compensation to make the legitimate transcendent disclosure of the masculine face of God the only expression of religious mystery. In Catholicism this spiritual flight from the earthly and feminine face of God led to many unfortunate tendencies.

One paradoxical modern tendency has been that the nearly exclusive stress on the masculine face of God has largely defined the religious dimension of the human in terms of the feminine symbol of receptivity, thus converting the church into a constituency made up by and large of women, and interpreting the largely masculine world of science and technology as "secular," meaning non-spiritual. (For example, I estimate that of the church audiences to which I speak, on the average approximately 70 per cent of the people present are women.) Thus the modern alienation of a "religious" church and a "secular" society can be perceived symbolically as the on-going process of female-male divorce.

But the unfortunate tendency with which I wish to begin here is the overall religious suppression of the regenerative spiritual power of the laity. This suppression in turn has led our Western church to its presently profound decline.

For example, certain spiritual teachers in the West said that to be holy "one must leave the world." This in turn led them to teach that the truly "religious" was to be found only outside creation, and that creation itself was "secular," by which these teachers meant devoid of spiritual depth. As a result, only certain Christians were named "religious," that is those who entered religious institutes and supposedly "left the world."

These "religious" were said to live in a "higher" way, a state of life different from and superior to the "lower" and "non-religious" way of the laity. By contrast, the state in life of the laity was implicitly judged by these spiritual teachers to be non-holy, non-religious, or secular because it was closely associated with the earth and its fertile sexuality, including woman.

The word secular comes from the Latin word *saeculum*, which means a cycle of time, an age or era. What makes an age a cycle is that it is subject to birth and then death, a sexual cycle of generation and degeneration. It should be no surprise then, that the root of the word *saeculum* is *secus*, whose variant is *sexus*, or sex.

Thus in Western spirituality the holy came to be defined as superior to the sexual cycle—as a non-regenerative way of life, gained by the passage through contemplation into the transcendent realm of the eternal and absolute. Many leaders in the the Western church tried exclusively to ground the church's identity on this legitimate but limited transcendent spirituality. The result was a church increasingly isolated from the immanent experience of the holy in the everyday life of its lay members.

Again one tragic result of this flight of spirituality from life—especially from the earth, sexuality, and the laity—was to paint science and technology as devoid of any immanent spiritual meaning. Yet this attempt backfired, for modern science and technology themselves became more masculine in character, and turned against its masculine theocratic competitor in the church's leadership. As a result, when science and technology became more powerful in our culture, they forced Western Christianity to give up its formerly dominant influence in society.

Two Catholic Reactions of Enabling

In reaction to this displacement from power, Catholicism followed two addictive patterns of response, one often episcopal and one often lay, with the presbyterate and religious shifting in between. On one side, which we might call masculine phallic competition, some modern Catholic episcopal leaders began to scold modern society for being "secular." As the technological power of modern society marginalized the church from its past theocratic role, this masculine side of the church grew resentful and ritualistically scapegoated society for in fact following through on the very secularization begun by Catholic spiritual teachers. This reaction may be described as the spirituality of *resentful transcendence*. Again, this reaction is more often found with the church's exclusively masculine leadership.

On the other side, which we might call feminine womb-like retreat, many modern Catholic laity began to enclose themselves spiritually within psychological interiority. Having defined ecology and society as outside the sphere of the holy, this side began to live in its own internal world as if the external world did not even exist. In place of scapegoating the outer world, it tended to ignore the wider world for its own self-absorption in a churchy sphere busy with liturgical life, religious education, fundraising, various committee meetings, or whatever. This may be described as the spirituality of *privatized interiority*. Again this reaction is more often found in the church's predominately largely feminine lay constituency.

A resentful scapegoating of the "secular" techno-scientific world by many masculine clerical leaders and a retreating into self- absorbed psychological privatization by the many largely feminine lay members are the twin codependent pathologies of Western Catholicism, in turn closely linked to the destructive anti-ecological addiction of Western culture. The clerically masculine form of church codependency angrily blames the crisis-ridden world, while the largely feminine lay form of church codependency pretends the crisis does not exist. One side is the punishing father, the other the permissive mother. (A third variant is angry scapegoating of the clerical leaders by "progressive" laity, religious, and clergy, but this is a weak third.)

Historically the modern masculine industrial rape of the feminine cycles of ecology was made spiritually permissible in the West only because some Western spiritual teachers had taught Western civilization to ground itself on symbolic flight from the the manifestation of God in the earth, in sexual energy, and particularly in the laity. That rape continues and now intensifies only because the masculine scapegoating resentment by church leaders of society in its moment of crisis and the feminine privatizing retreat of church members from this same social crisis continue to enable the anti-ecological addiction.

In a certain sense we might say that the church reaction of scapegoating imitates war, while the church reaction of privatization imitates abortion. One tries to kill life from the outside (throwing churchy bombs at the world), while the other tries to kill from the inside (keeping real evangelical mission from being born). In different ways but with the same result, both pathologies lead to a death of evangelical mission one by angrily rejecting the world, the other by hiding in fear from it.

Paradoxically, both sides of this loss of mission forget one of two sides of the New Testament's healing words of masculine love (letting go as on the Cross) and feminine power (birthing as in Pentecost) as the two faces of God. The masculine temptation of scapegoating forgets the Gospel's revelation of the loving dimension of the masculine face of God:

> *Yes, God so loved the world, that he gave his only Son. God did not send the Son into the world to condemn the world, but that the world might be saved through him. (John 3:16-17)*

Meanwhile, the feminine temptation to self-absorption forgets the Gospel's revelation of the powerful birthing dimension of the feminine face of God:

> *You will receive power when the Holy Spirit [in Hebrew the word for Spirit, Ruah, is feminine] comes down upon you; then you are to be my witnesses in Jerusalem, throughout Judea and Samaria, yes, even to the ends of the earth. (Acts 1:8)*

The Resulting Crisis of Catholicism in the West

The codependency of Western Catholicism with the anti-ecological addiction of Western Culture has led to the great late modern crisis of Western Catholicism—the progressive abandonment of the Catholic Church by the people of the West for other Christian bodies, for other religions, for the secular religion of Communism, or for no religion at all. This abandonment began with the Reformation, and was dramatically accelerated in the broad dechristianization which hit Western Europe during the last 100 years—particularly in France, Germany, and Italy. Today, in those three countries which constituted the heart of the classical Catholic evangelization, the Catholic Church has been dramatically weakened, with its surviving institutions continuing largely through government funding. In addition, in U.S. Catholicism we are now experiencing perhaps a 10 per cent defection rate, offset only by the influx of immigration and higher birth-rates of those among us who are not of European descent. Since the bulk of the new immigrants are Hispanic, there is no cause for security even in that area. Recent estimates suggest that the Catholic monopoly in Latin America is being aggressively challenged by more evangelical and lay-rooted evangelicals and pentecostals—with approximately 3 million converts per year. Already it is projected that the nation of Guatemala will be half Protestant by the end of this century.There have been important exceptions to the historical pattern of abandonment, and some church leaders and members have attempted to use these exceptions as a strategic model for Catholic re-evangelization of the West. For example, the European semi-periphery of Poland was temporarily spared dechristianization, because Catholicism served there as a national rallying symbol against the invading foreign and non-Catholic power of Russian Communism. The same nationalist pattern also temporarily buttressed Catholicism in the European semi- periphery of Ireland during the time of

English Protestant domination. The United States and Canada were also, until recently, spared Catholic dechristianization because these churches served European immigrants as both a defensive buffer against the surrounding hostile Protestant culture and as a offensive launching pad for their children into the new middle class.But we cannot presume that these exceptional patterns will last long in the new period of the West's acute ecological and spiritual crisis, nor can we presume that these exceptions will provide the model on a global scale for creative evangelical strategy. Already in Ireland, the process of dechristianization is rapidly advancing among the youth. The same negative process is well developed in once Catholic Quebec. It remains to be seen whether Poland, should it become semi-autonomous of Russia and fully open itself to the West, would sustain a broad Catholic presence. We already know that in Poland there seems little correlation between nationalist support for the institutional church and actual Catholic moral practice. For example, Poland apparently has the highest rates of abortion in the world. In addition, here in the United States, as we go further away from the period of the European immigrations (the so-called "immigrant church"), present tendencies suggest that dechristianization of Catholic youth in the U.S. will continue to advance.

Gifts of Hope

Yet the Holy Spirit is presently offering us resources for the crisis in a creative understanding of the spiritual power of earth, of the fertile embrace of woman and man, and of the church's vast lay base. The Holy Spirit wishes to use these gifts to heal Western culture of its anti-ecological addiction and to re-evangelize the Western Church from its pathological codependencies.

But, as the ecological crisis deepens, if Western Catholicism fails to open itself to these gifts of God, then the mutual breakdown of Western culture and of Western Catholicism—as conspiring addict and enabler—will only intensify. We could see for Western Catholicism continued loss of numbers and revenues, and a deepening of the two codependent pathologies. With a weak lay sense of spiritual power, we could see deeper lay (largely feminine) retreat into a spirituality of privatized interiority. With a culturally defensive masculine clerical leadership, we could see simultaneously deeper resentful scapegoatings of secularism and of all who cannot be controlled.All of this, of course, would only further feed the basic Western addiction to poisoning the earth—by intensifying through passive and active modes the West's spiritual flight from the earthly, lay-rooted, feminine/masculine faces of God. Lest this all appear too bleak, allow me now to turn to the third and hopeful part of this paper.

C. RE-EVANGELIZATION, THE LAITY, AND HOME MISSIONS

The point of the preceding analysis of addiction and the crisis of Western culture, as well as of Catholic complicity in it, has been to set a context a strategic call to look to the laity as the rich source of the healing re-evangelization of society—by the church at large and by Glenmary in particular. But in pointing to the laity, I do not wish to suggest that the laity are some magic Utopian solution out there just waiting to end Western culture's ecological addition or the Western church's institutional decline. Quite the contrary.

The Laity's Avoidance of Responsibility

My own organizing experience suggests that the laity

will be drawn into their full blown mission only slowly, and probably kicking and screaming in protest along the way—much like an addict being forced into a recovery program. Addicts do not wish to face their accountability for the spiritual power within them. They do not wish to admit that their own image is the image of God. Neither do any of us. Thus it is also with the Catholic laity. Recall that when Moses, in response to God's command and power, led the children of Israel out of their slavery in Egypt, the children of Israel did not thank Moses. Rather they complained to him,

> *Why did you do this to us? Why did you bring us out of Egypt? Did we not tell you this in Egypt, when we said, "Leave us alone, let us serve the Egyptians?" (Exodus 14:11-12).*

So will it be, I believe, with the laity's acceptance of their mission. Its birthing may occur only in anger and protest—perhaps as a wife sometimes curses her husband when the muscular contractions of childbirth reach their peak. "Why did you do this to me," the laity may bitterly lash out at those church leaders and staff, as well as other laity, who truly confront them with the terror of their spiritual power. By the way, this spiritual power comes not first from our being Christian, but from our humanity. The image of God in us is not first the Christian image but the human image. That image has been wounded by sin, but not destroyed. The purpose of the Gospel, of baptism, and of Christianity is not to substitute for our human spiritual power, but to heal it and to make it even more powerful.

If the church—meaning here the church as a separate social institution made up of leaders, staff, and part-time constituents—is where the enabling of Western culture's addiction to ecological destruction lies, then the addiction itself can be found in the laity's everyday life in society. The statement that the church is the enabler and society is the addict might be rephrased as the church's leadership and staff are the enablers, while the church's laity are the addicts. The root problem of Western culture's addiction is with the laity—particularly in degenerating forms of work life and family life. To challenge the laity's primary addiction, church leaders and staff professionals need first to cease enabling the laity's addiction, which brings me to what might be called the religious temptation as the basic form of churchy enabling.

The Danger of Religious RespectIt appears so much easier for the laity to let bishops, priests, deacons, religious Sisters and Brothers, and even lay ministers take exclusive responsibility for spiritual power. Then these roles can be described as "religious vocations." For, just as Jesus warned against, the laity will happily reward these poor unfortunate folks with long religious or academic titles, the first seats in holy places, awe and respect for their religious offices, and generous financial donations. The laity will say, "How different these religious people are from us—how much holier, or how much more intelligent, or how superior!" But the sad secret of such "praise and respect" is that the laity will thereby have freed themselves from their own terrifying responsibility for spiritual power. The laity will thereby be able to pretend that their everyday life is really not religious, and that only certain places and certain people are religious—but of course not our places and not ourselves. We laity will thereby free ourselves from accountability for our addiction to destroying the earth, and from all our parallel addictions as well.

This is why Jesus reserved his strongest anger not for sexual sinners like an adulteress or prostitute, nor for those like tax collectors or rich merchants who lusted after money, nor even for those like Pontius Pilate who seized such human power over life and death. No, as we remember from the Gospels, Jesus' greatest anger was for those religious leaders who believed that religious energy was centered in themselves and in their states in life. For these, Jesus said, the severest sentence will be given. (Mark 12:40) For Jesus knew that we would so easily surrender our spiritual power to a religious caste as a way of avoiding the terror of our own God-given spiritual responsibility.We certainly try hard to avoid this responsibility. Somehow we even manage to develop a language which cultivates the very dangers which Jesus set out to avoid. I speak particularly of our present human-invented and non-evangelical distinctions between religious and secular, and between clergy and laity. Before we can understand the spiritual power of the laity for today, we need first to break beyond the distortions of these anti-evangelical distinctions.

The Historical Emergence of a Religious Caste

The idea of a religious or clerical elite caste is as old as human civilization. In general, it seems that the high classical empires began with urban-based pagan warrior-priests who learned how to dominate various tribes around their cities, organize them into worship at their temples, conscript their labor, and take from them heavy taxes. One of the ways by which these warrior-priests justified their seizure of power was to say that their sphere of activities was sacred, while all else was profane. Profane in its Latin roots comes from *pro fanum* meaning "outside the temple." Thus what the pagan priests did in the temple was called sacred or religious, but what other people did outside the temple was called profane or secular.As the early civilizations developed, the originally ruling warrior-priest caste made the mistake of eventually letting others do their military dirtywork for them. Then it was not long before a military caste of warrior-nobles developed alongside the pagan priestly caste. Since the warrior-nobles now had the weapons, they turned the tables on the priests, took top power from them, and converted the pagan priests into their ideological servants. As a result of this priestly loss of power, a tendency rose up and remained among priestly groups in all civilizations to resent those in society who held the highest power, in place of themselves—in part an anti-technological resentment. So there has always been in human history this hidden and resentful clerical wish to regain control of all society. This is the first clerical temptation. To some degree it triumphed in Europe during the Middle Ages when bishoprics and monasteries became major centers of economic and military power.But when such triumph was not feasible, priestly groups have been tempted to compensate for their absence of economic and military power by puffing up their religious importance and by holding themselves religiously above others. That is the second clerical temptation. Apparently it was that way in Israel when Jesus came on the scene.Yet the biblical tradition was always uneasy with the sacred-profane distinction. Recall that Yahweh originally did not want Israel to build a temple, for fear it would become like the pagan nations. Later, after the temple had been built and become corrupt, King Josiah held the equivalent of Israel's Vatican II liturgical reform of the temple. But the prophet Jeremiah warned that liturgical reform of the temple alone was a shallow and even dangerous thing,

> *Put not your trust in the deceitful words, 'This is the Temple of the Lord! The Temple of the Lord! The Temple of the Lord!' (Jeremiah 7:4)*

Because Israel narrowed its religious consciousness to churchy things and so became idolatrous, Yahweh had foreign armies destroy the temple and send the people in the bitter suffering of exile, as Jeremiah had foretold. Still later, Jesus warned of the same danger, and the destruction of the second Jewish temple soon followed.

The Lay Teaching of Jesus

Jesus did not present himself in Israel as a priest. He was not born into one of the priestly families (like his cousin John), nor did he wear priests' robes. He severely criticized those religious leaders who made a public display of a distinctive religious image—by special titles, clothes, seats of honor, etc. Rather Jesus presented himself as a lay person—a teacher, yes, a rabbi, yes, but in Israel both those functions were lay. And he did so in a blatantly lay manner. To be still more careful that his followers not succumb to the religious temptation, Jesus insisted that they should not call any of their leaders by the titles of rabbi, teacher, or even father. Thus in the Gospel According to Matthew, we read,

> *As to you, avoid the title, 'Rabbi.' One among you is the teacher, the rest are learners. Do not call anyone on earth your father. Only one is your father, the One in heaven. Avoid being called teachers. Only one is your teacher, the Messiah. (Matthew 23:8-10)*

Right after that in Matthew's Gospel comes Jesus' strongest dennunciation of the religious leaders for setting themselves above the people. By contrast, Jesus' own teaching stressed that all people in Israel were chosen as the salt of the earth, the light of the world, a holy nation, a priestly people, as indeed the Hebrew Scriptures had taught.

The word that the translators of the Hebrew scriptures into Greek had used to describe this chosen, holy, royal, and priestly people was the word, *laos*, from which we derive our term "laity." The word "laity" thus means God's own chosen, holy, royal, and priestly people. The words "religious" and "priestly" are generally not used in the New Testament apart from laity, because they are contained in the laity.

The Lay Experience of the Early Church

When Christianity was separated from the synagogue, this idea of the chosenness, holiness, royalness, and priestliness of the laity was applied by Jesus' followers to the church, meaning the full community of Jesus' disciples. They understood themselves as a holy nation, a priestly people. In that sense the word "laity" is simply an interchangeable term for the word "church." How often have I been told by well-intentioned people that we should eliminate the word "laity," because it is so demeaning. Just the opposite. We need to eliminate the words "clergy" and "religious" to discover the spiritual depth of the word "laity."There were many offices and charisms in the early lay community of Jesus' disciples—especially the episcopate, the presbyterate and the diaconate, as well as prophets, healers, etc. These were offices and charisms with real power—for example the *episcopos* or bishop was the real leader of the community of disciples, with real authority, though he was forbidden by the Gospel from lording this authority over the community or from making himself seem important. In addition, there was no thought that for religious reasons such lay leaders of the community would not be married. The witness of celibacy was treasured within the early Christian community, but it was not seen as a requirement for a special clerical or religious caste. Rather it was to be found where the Spirit willed it—randomly within the full community of disciples. In fact, the presumption for the episcopal leaders of the community was just the opposite, namely that they would be married. So in the New Testament, we read,

> A *bishop must be married only once . . . keeping his own children under control . . . for if a man does not know how to manage his own house, how can he take care of the Church of God. (Second Thessalonians, 3:2 5)*

This quote, if nothing else, should make it clear to us that the Gospel has no place for the religious-secular distinction, which is based on the non-evangelical view that the sexual realm is somehow below the holy. So it was too that Peter, the first bishop of Rome, was married, and reportedly for centuries the Christians of Rome remembered his daughter Petronilla (i.e. little female Peter) as one of their favorite saints.These important offices and charisms were all understood as within the laity, not outside them. Above all there was no special dress, or honor, or title for these people. In the apostolic church, Peter had no title but Peter. John no title but John, etc. There were no holinesses nor eminences, nor most reverends, right reverends, very reverends, nor even unadorned plain old reverends. Peter, John and the others would have been embarrassed by anyone who used such terms, and probably would have become angry at them for so threatening the Gospel. In the fundamental biblical sense, to distinguish by levels of honor or the holiness of states in life the laity from the clergy, or even levels within clergy, or later so to distinguish "religious" from "seculars," or even "religious priests" from "secular priests" is a clear confusion of the evangelical good news. There were of course the titles "sister" and "brother"— not for "professed religious" but for all in the community of disciples.In this way, following Jesus' instructions, the apostolic church made sure that all the disciples knew that the spiritual power of the Gospel was their personal power and their personal responsibility. If some individuals did not feel sure of that power, it was only because they had not yet received the special gift of the Spirit, which is boldness. But that was solved by praying over them and asking the Spirit to come upon them with her gift of boldness. Thus lay boldness rather than religious honor was the loving power of the early and evangelical church.(Note: Clericalism is something entirely different from the Catholic understanding of orders. The Catholic faith insists that the leadership offices of bishop, presbyter, and deacon all have a sacramental, or as sometimes stated in Platonic language, an ontological character. But the social trappings of clericalism have nothing to do with this sacramental character. Rather, I would argue, clericalism actually hinders the evangelical power of sacramental offices.)

Subsequent Confusions and Healing Reforms

Later, with the appropriation of Greco-Roman imperial administrative forms of pagan religion, the word "clergy" was introduced into the Christian vocabulary and then counterposed to the word "laity." That development coincided with the elevation of the community's lay leaders into a distinct religious caste. Bishops and later presbyters granted special social privileges by imperial Roman law, as had been the case in the Empire with pagan priests. Eventually many of these "clergy," and especially the bishops among them, would be corrupted by the political power and financial wealth given to them in the late Roman Empire. In reaction to this early clerical corruption of the leaders of the community of Jesus' disciples, a movement of reform grew up. This was the originally lay movement of monasticism—whereby some lay disciples abandoned the corruption of the of the urban church of the Roman cities and went out to the desert, as Israel and Jesus had done before them. Over time, their reform had an enormous influence on the urban church, such that a tradition developed that it was better to chose one's bishop from these reforming lay disciples in the desert, rather than from the often corrupt urban clergy.Over time, however, as the monasteries grew wealthy, these lay monks themselves also wished to be clericalized, such that today monasticism appears to us as a clerical rather than lay movement. Yet even the prayer of the hours, which we consider a clerical or religious prayer, was originally a Jewish lay prayer, taken over from the synagogue where lay people, often elderly retired men, gathered throughout the day to pray the psalms of David.When monasticism lost much of its original spiritual power, new lay movements of renewal again developed to teach us the original vision of the Gospel. Perhaps the most dramatic of these has been the Franciscan movement. Approximately 800 years ago, a young man named Giovanni Francesco Bernadone gathered around himself some others and originally called their little band the "brothers of the lower class," or on other occasions "the men of penance from Assisi." Today, in our typical obscuring of the biblical vision, we make Francis's followers sound "religified"—meaning something strange and distant from everyday Christians. Instead of the clear and simple translation of his group's name as "brothers of the lower class," we now use the latinization, "friars minor." (*Menores*, from which comes the latinization *minor*, was the class term used in Francis' time to name the lower class of the poor.)When even Francis' movement was religified and clericalized, he still turned to those who still knew themselves as lay to create what others would later call the "Third Order." The term "order" comes from imperial Roman administrative language, and means in effect a social class. Thus a lay third order would mean the third class down the social (or in this case spiritual) ladder. In that sense an "order" at the bottom of the spiritual ladder is paradoxically truest to Francis' deeply evangelical sense that the first shall be last and the last first. But Francis never called this group a third order, but rather "the brothers (and sisters) of penance"—the very name he had given to his original group in Assisi.

As we can now see, perhaps the central axis of reform in the church throughout its history is the choice between these two alternatives:

The Imperial/Medieval Clericalist Model: clericalizing and religifying caste elites who are then portrayed as above the community of lay Christians, in effect suppressing the evangelical power of the laity and returning to the model of clergy and religious as above the laity, a model intensified by the economic and military power of bishoprics and monasteries in the Middle Ages; or

The Apostolic Lay Model: a return to the apostolic model of a lay community containing within it various ministries, including the ministry of the ordained—in effect letting clerical and religious pretensions fall from false power into the warm embrace of the Holy Spirit amidst the full lay community of Jesus's disciples where we remember together that we are all responsible for the love and power of the Gospel.

When this rediscovery of the lay character of the entire church happens, then the laos vastly increases its evangelical energy. But when this lay-rootedness is confused and forgotten, then the laos is drained of evangelical energy; when the church losses this lay energy, then the mission grows weak. Yet when this lay-rooted evangelical flows, then the church's mission grows strong.If the present sinful and destructive addictions of Western culture are to be evangelically challenged, particularly the acute threat to the entire ecosystem, then we need to overcome the enabling religious temptations to suppress the spiritual power of the laity. For all the Spirit-filled boldness of the full laos is needed for the re-evangelization of the West.

The Various Tendencies of the Present Moment

We are once again at a crossroads in the Western church. It appears that, in the new cultural transition, the false power of clericalism and of religiosity is again fading. But the death of clericalism is not the same as the death of the ministry of the ordained bishops, presbyters, and deacons, nor of evangelical intentional communities. To unleash their charisms as servants of the spiritual boldness of the laos, it is necessary first to cast aside this clericalism and religiosity. So far, in our present cultural transition, it seems that we have many distinct tendencies flowing among us all at once—some creative, some destructive, many ambiguous:

Neo-Clericalism: One dangerous tendency is a neo-clericalism—the attempt to protect fading cleric status and even to expand its false power. This is often the perspective behind those who think that everything will be solved if only we can get back up the number of "clerical and religious vocations." This triumphalist distortion fails to understand Jesus' teaching in the New Testament. Of course we need more personnel for these offices and charisms of the laos, so the problem is not with the search for personnel. Rather the problem is with the religious temptation sometimes guiding the search.

Lay Professionalism: A second dangerous tendency

is to think that professionalization of lay ministries will solve the problem. We should welcome and clearly need countless more lay ministers, including ones who are well prepared professionally. The danger here is not with lay ministries themselves, nor with professional training, but with a new temptation to replace a clerical caste with a professional caste, and still not to turn in a fundamental way to the spiritual power of the laity.

Lay Privatization: A third dangerous tendency is deepening spiritual privatization—a spiritual renewal which turns the laity inward only toward church activities, or points them outward but only in terms of ethics. The problem here is not the church activities or ethics per se, but the failure to understand the sacred character of society in its work and family life, in its science and technology, in its economics, politics and culture, and indeed the sacred character of the entire universe, and to see these as mediators of the fundamental disclosure of the Word of God. Two ambiguous but potentially creative tendencies, I believe, are both the reforms among many religious orders to link themselves with the laity, and the birth of new lay movements of renewal, for example Opus Dei, charismatic covenant communities, Communio e Liberazione, etc.

Lay-Bonding Projects of Religious Congregations: These are to be praised for looking to the laity. But the goal and power of that looking becomes questionable when it is designed to associate laity with religious, rather than the reverse. In some cases, I have the impression that at least the language of bonding projects places the particular charism of the order in a more central position than the Gospel of Jesus Christ. Thus sometimes such literature invites lay people to join the religious in the institute's charism, rather than asking them through the institute's charism to serve the Gospel of Jesus Christ—into which laity have already been baptized. Wherever this danger is present, there would be a turn to lay energy, but only to protect the religious temptation.

New Lay Movements: These are rich new examples of earlier waves of lay-inspired renewals of the community of Jesus's disciples. In this sense, they may be one of the great hopes of the future of Catholicism. But presently sometimes they paradoxically appear to support a clericalist view of church linked not to the normative vision of the New Testament, but to the imperial/Medieval clerical distortions. Wherever this danger is present, movements would be drawing on the rich treasury of lay energy, but then orienting it to serve the clerical temptation.

Finally, there are countless hopeful signs that many of Jesus disciples be they called clerical, religious, or lay—are recovering the boldness of the Holy Spirit to share the Good News with the full community of disciples, with family and friends, and with all the earth. This Good News which Jesus brought tells us:

> *That God's good, yet wounded creation is being healed in Jesus, and that in that healing God's spiritual power in us is deepened;*
>
> *That through this power both individual persons and corporate social structures, and even the threatened ecological structure of the earth, can be liberated from the addictive destruction of sin;*
>
> *That this liberation comes from our remembering that we are made in the female and male images of God, and that our spiritual creativity flows from the communion in us of those two Divine images; and*
>
> *That in this spiritual power, we care deeply in love and power about the earth which is presently being poisoned, and about so many of our youth who are*

also being poisoned.

Concluding Reflection For Glenmary

It has not been my goal in this address to tell Glenmary how to use the "Evangelizing Role of the Catholic Laity in the Home Missions," but simply to tell you of its power and of the need for it. There are within and around Glenmary individuals far more creative than I for designing programs to tap lay spiritual energy for the new evangelization. But evangelical conversion comes first; then evangelical programs can follow. If the conversion is truly evangelical, then the programs will be spiritually powerful. If the conversion is not truly evangelical, then the programs will be still-born. Were that to happen, then I fear that the first and pessimistic scenario would prevail for Glenmary—decline and perhaps even death. In its history Glenmary has been a rich carrier of evangelical energy. Now it is time to risk carrying even more—in and through the laity. If Glenmary fears for its future and tries to protect its dwindling resources according to the neo-clerical strategy, then as Jesus taught us in trying to save its life, Glenmary could well loose it. But if Glenmary is willing to risk its future with the laity, then—as Jesus taught us—in giving up clerical security, it will gain fresh life. If that happens, then the optimistic scenarios could prevail. Then all the church would be blessed with the spiritual energy that will flow forth from Glenmary across the home missions. Such an evangelical lay opening of Glenmary would, I believe, draw to Glenmary's missionary efforts many Hispanic-Americans and African-Americans * themselves so much more aware than European Americans of the spiritual power of the laity. It would also propose that such new lay-rooted spiritual energy, particularly in rural areas, could prove—in ways we have yet to imagine—an important part of healing of our deep anti-ecological and therefore anti-rural addiction.

Come Holy Spirit,
send forth your Spirit and we shall be recreated,
and you through Glenmary in the full power of the laity
shall renew the face of the home missions.

CONTRIBUTORS

Joseph Cardinal Bernardin is the Archbishop of Chicago. He served as the president of the National Conference of Catholic Bishops from 1974 to 1977, and is a recognized spokesperson for the church in America on pastoral issues.

Joe Holland is a Catholic theologian specializing in the relationship of theology and social analysis. He works as an independent lecturer and writer. He has published five books including one written with Peter Henriot, **Social Analysis: Linking Faith and Justice**.

Bill Leonard is Professor of Church History, The Southern Baptist Theological Seminary. He has lectured widely on religion in American. His books include **Word of God Across the Ages** (1981), **Out of One, Many: American Religion and American Pluralism** (1984), and **The Nature of the Church** (1986).

Jamie Phelps, O.P., is Assistant Professor of Doctrinal Theology, Catholic Theological Union. Her interests focus on issues affecting African-Americans, women and the Third World. She is a frequent speaker at regional and national workshops.

John S. Rausch resides at the Glenmary Research Center in Atlanta where he writes and participates in educational workshops on economics and religion.

Frank Ruff is the president of the Glenmary Home Missioners. Devoted to ecumenism, he served as the Catholic representative to the Catholic-Baptist dialogue. He also served as coordinator for Region 5 of the Conference of Major Superiors of Men.

Sr. Yolanda Tarango, C.C.V.I. is a member of the Sisters of the Incarnate Word from San Antonio. She is a nationally known lecturer on Hispanic Catholicism. Sr. Yolanda was a staff member of the Mexican American Cultural Center in San Antonio and is presently national coordinator of *Las Hermanas*. In addition, she has co-authored a book with Ada Maria Isasi-Diaz entitled **Hispanic Women: Prophetic Voice in the Church**